P9-CDW-271

Kurt Cobain

"Oh Well, Whatever, Nevermind"

Read about other

American REBELS

Jack Kerouac
"The Road Is Life"

0-7660-2448-2

Jimi Hendrix
"Kiss The Sky"

0-7660-2449-0

James Dean
"Dream As If You'll Live Forever"

0-7660-2537-3

Madonna
"Express Yourself"

0-7660-2442-3

American REBELS

Kurt Cobain

"Oh Well, Whatever, Nevermind"

Jeff Burlingame

Enslow Publishers, Inc.
40 Industrial Road
Box 398
Berkeley Heights, NJ 07922
USA
http://www.enslow.com

Library of Congress Cataloging-in-Publication Data:

Burlingame, Jeff.
Kurt Cobain : "oh well, whatever, nevermind" / Jeff Burlingame.
p. cm. — (American rebels)
Includes bibliographical references and index.
ISBN-10: 0-7660-2426-1
1. Cobain, Kurt, 1967–1994—Juvenile literature. 2. Nirvana (Musical group)—Juvenile literature. 3. Rock musicians—United States—Biography—Juvenile literature. I. Title. II. Series.
ML3930.C525B87 2006
782.42166092—dc22
[B]

2006001742

ISBN-13: 978-0-7660-2426-7

Printed in the United States of America

10 9 8 7 6 5 4 3 2

To Our Readers: We have done our best to make sure all Internet Addresses in this book were active and appropriate when we went to press. However, the author and the publisher have no control over and assume no liability for the material available on those Internet sites or on other Web sites they may link to. Any comments or suggestions can be sent by e-mail to comments@enslow.com or to the address on the back cover.

Illustration Credits: Associated Press/AP, pp. 67, 110; Getty Images, pp. 6, 98, 121; Jeff Burlingame, pp. 25, 133; Leland Cobain, pp. 16, 17, 85, 91; Photos.com, pp. 37, 59; © S.I.N./CORBIS, pp. 49, 56; Time Life Pictures/Getty Images, pp. 75, 89.

Cover Illustration: Getty Images

Contents

Kurt Cobain performs during the taping for *Unplugged* on November 18, 1993.

Live and Not Loud

The dimly lit set was eerie. Filled with candles and lilies, the small stage at Sony Studios in New York City looked more like a funeral than the setting of an important rock concert.

This was exactly the way Kurt Cobain wanted it to be.

The abnormally tranquil musicians did little to alter the morose mood of the chilly November night, but those calm appearances were just a front. Although they had played in front of thousands of fans each night, the members of Nirvana were worried about MTV's intimate *Unplugged* show because many critics did not think the band would perform well there. The name of the show was *Unplugged* because bands were supposed to use acoustic guitars and play quietly. Nirvana was famous for being an alternative rock and roll band with electric guitars and big amplifiers playing at full volume.

This was an entirely different environment from the big arena shows Nirvana was used to. The show's producer said, "They were really nervous about doing *Unplugged*. Because they were really leaving themselves wide open."[1]

It turned out there was no need to worry. The crowd applauded and whistled passionately after each hit Nirvana played, and Cobain's confidence subtly grew with each cheer. With only two words left in the fourteenth and final song, Cobain paused to take a breath before finishing.

Singing, "Where Did You Sleep Last Night?" with the camera zoomed in on his face, Cobain sighed, opening his brilliant blue eyes to gaze out above the small crowd. Closing his eyes again, he howled the final words, then strummed his guitar as he and the rest of Nirvana finished the tune. Waving to the crowd, Cobain said, "Thank you," and the show was over. The audience applauded wildly and waited for one more song. But Cobain was spent. The producer said, "I tried to talk the band into doing another song as an encore. . . . But Kurt felt like he was done. I think at that moment he realized that this was amazing."[2]

Cobain sighed, opening his brilliant blue eyes to gaze out above the small crowd.

The band was relieved while watching a tape of the performance immediately after the show. They were pleased they had pulled off what many thought they could not do. In the days following, people were talking about what a triumph the show was. It went on to win a Grammy Award for Best Alternative Music Performance and is considered one of the most successful shows of Nirvana's career. It may not have been as loud and wild as normal, but it was groundbreaking for showing another side of Cobain's songwriting many had not seen.

Prior to *Unplugged*, it was mostly teenagers and young adults who loved Nirvana's music. That age group bought millions of the band's CDs and made Nirvana extremely popular throughout the world. Many older adults could not relate to what Cobain was singing. They thought the band was too loud and often said the music was a trend that would quickly pass. Adults of past eras had said the same thing about risk-taking musicians of their time, like Elvis Presley and the Beatles.

Cobain's grandfather, Leland Cobain, had every Nirvana album, but was one of those who never understood what his grandson was singing. Watching the *Unplugged* show helped him better identify with his grandson's way of thinking. "I'm from the '30s and '40s," he said. "I listened to Glenn Miller. But when I seen Kurt on the MTV with just him and the guitar, I liked that. Without all those drums beating and the noise I could finally understand him."[3]

Cobain and his band have been on the cover of hundreds of magazines and newspapers since the

Unplugged show. They were on hundreds more before then. Through it all, Cobain struggled with the popularity of being recognized by the public and scrutinized by the media. He always wanted to be a rock star but when he became one he realized it was not as great as he thought it would be. Suddenly the whole world wanted to be his friend, and he had no privacy. He said, "I didn't know how to deal with it. If there was a Rock Star 101 course, I would have liked to take it. It might have helped me."[4]

"If there was a Rock Star 101 course, I would have liked to take it."

Cobain's blue eyes have been talked about countless times since the 1993 *Unplugged* show. He rarely opened his eyes wide when he sang and during *Unplugged* he sang most of "Where Did You Sleep Last Night?" with his eyes focused down on his guitar and sheet music. That is why many people noticed when he opened them for two brief seconds near the end. Some said Cobain looked scared and some thought he looked sad. Others believed his eyes told a silent story of an unhappy man.

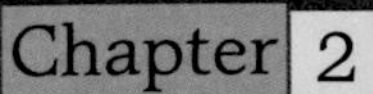

Chapter 2 Metamorphosis

Boys' flannel shirts were two for $3 in Aberdeen, Washington, on February 20, 1967. Wool sweaters were just $2 and a pocket radio was $2.22, batteries and headphones included. Each of those items would later hold much significance for Don and Wendy Cobain's first child, but the young couple did not care much about sales on this day. The Cobains were busy at Grays Harbor Community Hospital. On a hill at the edge of town, high above the city's stores and traffic, Wendy Cobain was giving birth to her first child, Kurt Donald Cobain.

Kurt's earliest days were spent with his parents in a tiny rental home in Hoquiam, a smaller city adjacent to Aberdeen. Wendy Cobain took care of Kurt while Don Cobain worked days at a gas station. When Kurt was six months old, the family moved to Aberdeen. Roughly twice the size of Hoquiam, Aberdeen and its nineteen thousand residents relied heavily on natural resources for income. In both towns, blue-collar jobs like logging were how many earned a living. The cities' names made that fact abundantly clear. Hoquiam is an Indian name meaning, "hungry for wood." Aberdeen's name is Scottish and means, "the meeting of two rivers."

Those two rivers, the Wishkah and Chehalis, are the reason early pioneers settled in Aberdeen. Long before paved roads covered the countryside, rivers were one of the main ways wood was shipped. Both the Wishkah and the Chehalis allowed for easy transport of logs to the nearby Pacific Ocean and points beyond. Before Kurt was born, several generations made excellent livings from harvesting the area's tree-filled forests.

At three, Kurt created his first song.

Kurt's family did not have a lot of money but were well known in the area. Many of his relatives were musical and young Kurt delighted in joining in wherever he could. His uncle, Chuck Fradenburg, was an accomplished local musician and his Aunt Mari played guitar. His great-uncle Delbert Fradenburg was a singer who had even been in a movie called, *The King of Jazz*.[1] So it did not surprise anyone when, at age two, Kurt began to show an interest in music. He began by singing popular Beatles songs like "Hey Jude" and toying with his aunt's guitar, holding it backwards because he was left-handed.[2] At three, Kurt created his first song. It went, "Corn on the cops, corn on the cops! The cops are coming! They're going to kill you."[3] Kurt said years later, "Every time I saw a cop I'd start singing that at them and pointing at them and telling them that they were evil. I didn't like them at all."[4] No one knew the reason for his distaste of police.

The same year Kurt wrote his first song, his sister, Kimberly, was born. With her blonde hair and fair complexion, she looked a lot like Kurt. Like many kids, young Kurt also had an imaginary friend. He named him Boddah and the two went everywhere together. The family eventually grew concerned with Kurt's fascination with Boddah and wanted to get rid of the pretend friend. Kurt's uncle Clark, who was in the military, came up with the solution. He took Boddah away to serve with him.

Kurt's grandfather remembers his grandson's early love of music exhibiting itself in many ways. Leland Cobain said, "Every time he used to come visit, he'd pound on all our pots and pans with a couple of pieces of kindling."[5] Fortunately for grandpa and grandma, Aunt Mari bought Kurt a real bass drum when he was seven, saving the family's cookware from more torture.

In addition to music, young Kurt showed a talent for visual arts, especially drawing. His grandfather tells the story of when "He come over to the house one day and said, 'Look, Grandpa. Look at the picture of Mickey Mouse I drew.' I looked at it and said, 'You didn't draw that, you traced it.' He got madder than heck. He said, 'I did not. Give me a piece of paper and I'll show ya.'"[6] Kurt's grandmother, Iris Cobain, handed Kurt some drawing paper and a felt pen. Leland Cobain continued,

"He said, 'I ain't gonna draw a Mickey Mouse because you said I traced it. I'll draw a Donald Duck.' And then he drew a Donald Duck and then he drew a Goofy and he said, 'There!'"[7]

Kurt was not only determined but also hyperactive and was prescribed Ritalin when he was seven. Ritalin is a somewhat controversial drug commonly given to kids to help increase their attention spans and decrease restlessness. Some argue against giving Ritalin to children, saying it makes them dependent on it and leads to other drugs later in life. Kurt also used some of his extra energy to compete in sports, just as his father had. He soon joined his first little league baseball team. Kurt's family members say he seemed disinterested in sports but still competed well.

It is hard to imagine an event occurring in elementary school changing someone's life forever, but most believe that is what happened to Kurt. When he was nine, his parents went through an emotional separation and soon divorced. Though he later called the divorce "a bore" in one of his songs, the happy kid who entertained everyone he came in contact with changed.

Divorce was a lot less common in the 1970s. Being a kid from a split family was often shameful and embarrassing. Young Kurt felt both of those emotions, saying later, "I didn't feel like I deserved to be hanging out with other kids, because they had parents and I didn't anymore."[8] On his bedroom wall, Kurt wrote,

"I hate Mom, I hate Dad, Dad hates Mom, Mom hates Dad, it simply makes you want to be sad."[9] Next to the depressing poem he drew pictures of his parents.[10]

For a year, Kurt and his sister continued living with their mother in their small Aberdeen home, valued by the courts at twenty thousand dollars. Don Cobain, who did not want the divorce, rented a small apartment in Hoquiam. Leland Cobain remembered, "Donnie was so darn shook up about it. For a long time, he thought they'd go back together."[11] That did not happen and the divorce became official in the summer of 1976. Wendy Cobain got to keep her eight-year-old Chevrolet Camaro sports car. Don Cobain kept his eleven-year-old Ford pickup and was ordered to pay $150 child support each month for Kurt and an equal amount for his sister.

Long fed up with a lack of attention from the sports-focused Don Cobain, good-looking Wendy Cobain was ready to move on and quickly found a new boyfriend. Don Cobain left Hoquiam and moved a few miles away just outside the small town of Montesano, first moving in with his parents, Leland and Iris Cobain, then to a manufactured home in the same trailer park. Most of the homes there were well kept and the yards were nicely trimmed.

Kurt did not get along with his mother's new boyfriend and soon went to live with his father. At first it was great. Kurt and his dad became instant pals, going fishing, camping, and to baseball games. Kurt was happy again, but that changed when his father started dating and eventually remarried. Don Cobain's new wife brought her own children into the household, and father and son were no longer alone. Kurt's new stepfamily meant he was not the center of his dad's attention. Kurt was even fine with sharing his dad until Don Cobain began favoring his new wife and stepkids. Leland Cobain said:

> I think he bent over backwards to please her and please her kids. I told Don, "You're gonna lose that kid. You can't treat Kurt like that. If you had an apple lying on a table, one of her kids could take a bite out of it and you wouldn't say a word to them. Kurt could take a bite out of it and you'd bat him alongside the head."[12]

A smiling Kurt at age thirteen.

The combined family needed a bigger home and moved inside the Montesano city limits. While living there, Kurt played drums in his elementary and junior high school bands, joined the wrestling team, and started dating his first girlfriend. According to one biographer, Kurt even made his own short films using his family's video camera. They were not happy tales. One was called *Kurt Commits Bloody Suicide*, where he pretended to cut his wrists with a torn pop

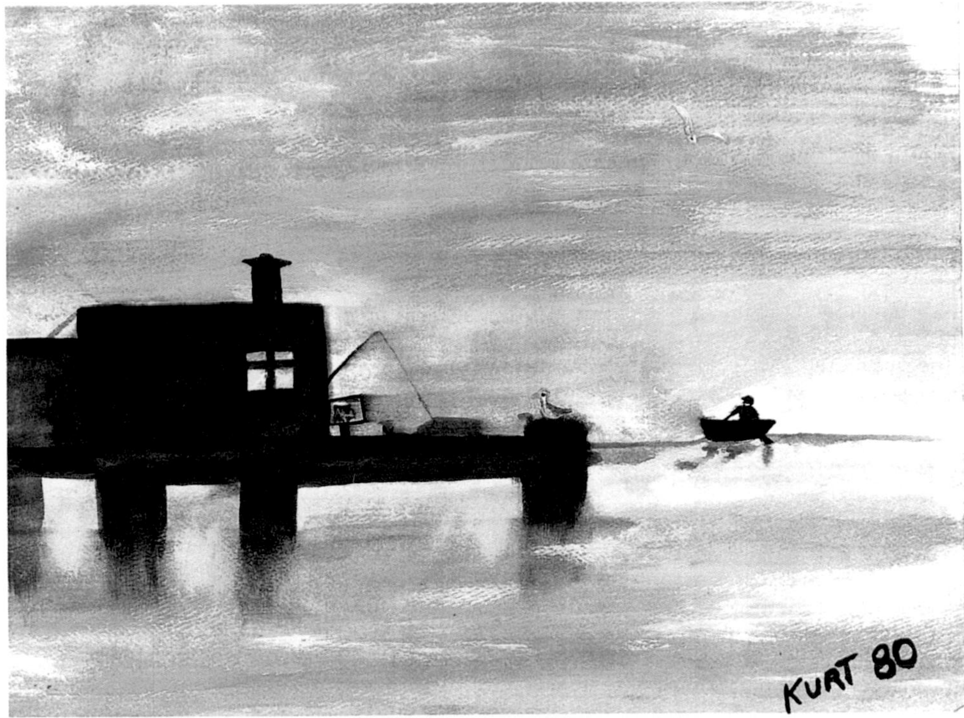

Above are two creations Kurt made in 1980, at the age of twelve or thirteen. At the top is a Christmas card he drew for his grandparents. At the bottom is an original painting.

can and bleed to death.[13] Although his musical skills were not especially developed, Kurt professed to one of his friends, "I'm going to be a superstar musician, kill myself, and go out in a flame of glory."[14]

Now spending more time away from home, Kurt first tried marijuana when he was fourteen. (Marijuana is an illegal drug that should be avoided.) It was the same year he got his first electric guitar from his uncle Chuck Fradenburg, the drummer in guitar teacher Warren Mason's band, called Fat Chance. The band practiced in Fradenburg's basement. That is where Mason first met Kurt. Mason recalled, "There was a little blonde-haired kid in the corner who was real quiet. Chuck asked later if I'd give him lessons if he paid me."[15] Mason agreed. The guitar Kurt brought to his first lesson was unplayable. The teacher remembered, "The neck was out of whack and it was unfixable."[16] So he ordered Kurt a guitar—a Gibson Explorer copy. He fixed it up a bit and set it up for Kurt. Because Kurt was left-handed, the strings had to be flipped around so he could strum with his left hand. Mason sold Kurt the guitar for $125.

Each week, Kurt paid five dollars for one half-hour lesson. Before the first one, Kurt told the teacher he already knew how to play the simple song "Louie, Louie." Kurt showed the teacher, incorrectly using just one string. Mason showed Kurt how to play the song properly and asked Kurt what his goals were. Kurt said he wanted to play "Stairway to Heaven," a classic song by the heavy metal band Led Zeppelin.[17] Kurt later denied saying that but Mason swears it is true. Kurt also said he wanted to learn how to write songs. The guitar teacher showed him some basic exercises. Some of them—especially a classic song structure called tension and release—showed up in many of Kurt's future songs.

Mason did not see any exceptional talent with Kurt but said the teen loved playing the guitar and practiced all the time. Kurt said years later, "As soon as I got my guitar, I just became so obsessed with it. . . . I knew I had something to offer and I knew eventually I would have the opportunity to show people I could write good songs."[18] He also knew practicing was how to get to that point. Kurt said, "I wasn't thriving socially, so I stayed in my room and played guitar all the time."[19] Kurt later told many people he had only taken one guitar lesson. Mason said that is not true and Kurt took lessons for about three months. His parents made him quit, the guitar teacher said, when he stopped doing his homework and only wanted to play the instrument. Kurt wanted to play his songs for people, but first wanted to join a band. In the meantime, he jammed with whomever he could.

On the Move

Kurt was unhappy at home and became a problem teen. He moved out of his dad's house to stay with various relatives and friends. He spent some time living with his grandparents, where he helped build an elaborate dollhouse for his grandma and carved a chess set for himself. For the latter project, Kurt took some leftover wood scraps from his grandpa's shop and meticulously drew designs on them and began whittling away with a knife. Seeing Kurt doing this, Leland Cobain decided to show him how to use a jigsaw, a saw with a thin blade used to cut curvy lines. It helped Kurt finish the job more quickly.

As fidgety teens often do, Kurt quickly grew bored. Leland Cobain told Kurt his friends could come visit but Kurt always said the eight miles from Aberdeen and two miles from Montesano were too far for anyone to travel, considering none of his friends had a driver's license. A lack of spending money was also an excuse Kurt used for not visiting friends.

To remedy this, his grandfather offered Kurt a job mowing the lawn for five dollars. Kurt wanted more money but Grandpa did not budge. Kurt finally accepted, and Leland Cobain cranked the engine of the push lawnmower, saying, "Watch that bag. When it gets full, empty the bag. He was a little perturbed about having to earn the money, I guess. I came in the house and sat there for a while and thought I'd look and see how he's doing."[20] Smoke was flying from the lawnmower and Kurt's grandpa rushed outside to see what was going on. He asked Kurt what he was doing. Kurt said he was cutting the grass, and his grandpa said, "Shut it off before you burn the engine up."[21] The lawnmower's grass-storage bag was so full no more would go in. Leland Cobain emptied it and Kurt continued mowing. Grandpa waited a little while then,

"I looked out the window again and it was the same thing. I went out there and I told him that's it. I gave him his $5 and said, 'I'll do it myself.'"[22] Kurt happily took the money, walked to the nearby highway, and caught a bus into Aberdeen.

For his sophomore year of high school, Kurt moved back to Aberdeen to live with his mother. For the most part, Aberdeen High School's social classes were split into three groups: the good students, the partiers, and the athletes. Those somewhere in-between, which is where Kurt fell, often felt left out. Kurt was intelligent, but his poor grades did not reflect it. He had begun smoking marijuana but did not have much else in common with those who hung around the "smoker's shed." And though he had done okay the previous year on Montesano High School's track team, he did not participate in sports when he transferred to Aberdeen High. That left Kurt an outcast in search of an identity. He had been popular at Montesano but did not have many close friends at his new school. He later wrote he "never had any friends because I hated everyone for they were so phony."[23]

One friend Kurt did have in Aberdeen was Myer Loftin. Myer and Kurt enjoyed the same type of music and began hanging out a lot. Myer eventually confessed to Kurt that he was gay. Kurt started getting teased and treated badly by kids for hanging around Myer. Kurt did not mind. He said later, "I started being proud of the fact that I was gay even though I wasn't."[24] What Kurt meant by this was that, even though he was not gay, he did not care if people thought he was.

Art was one area Kurt had never stopped excelling in. His teacher, Bob Hunter, said, "It was obvious from my first meeting with Kurt that he was gifted. Only time would prove how multi-dimensional he was at visual art, writing, and playing musical instruments."[25] Artistically, Kurt was far ahead of most high school students. One of his drawings was called "Metamorphosis" and showed twelve scenes of a sperm turning into a baby. His art teacher said it was, "very remarkable for a person of 16 to accomplish."[26]

Kurt also painted his own version of "American Gothic" by Grant Wood. Wood's original painting showed a woman and a man in front of a farmhouse with the man holding a pitchfork. In his version, Kurt replaced the heads of the farmers with the heads of punk rockers and won an award for the painting at an art show. Many writers have said Kurt won a college scholarship for art but his teacher says that was not true because Kurt never graduated.[27] Hunter said Kurt was, "quiet, introspective, super creative, and had a great sense of humor."[28] Although it was a visual art class, the subject of music came up now and again because Hunter played the radio when class was in session. Aberdeen's limited selection of radio stations often did not agree with Kurt. The teacher said, "A constant request of his was to turn off Top 40 rock and put something else on."[29]

Meeting the Melvins

Nearly as important to his life path as his parents' divorce had been years earlier was Kurt's discovery of the Melvins, a successful local rock band. The Melvins were playing concerts in much-larger areas like Seattle and Olympia, the liberal Washington State capital city, fifty miles from Aberdeen. Their music was unlike anything Kurt had heard. It was far different from the popular rock and roll records he had grown up listening to and heard on the radio, in art class or elsewhere. The Melvins played a slowed-down music with heavy guitar sounds. The band's pounding drums and bass guitar shook the listener's body when the volume was cranked up and their singer roared his lyrics.

The Melvins' singer/guitarist was a charismatic and outspoken Afro-haired Montesano man named Roger "Buzz" Osborne. Osborne said of the time:

> All the bands I knew or heard in Aberdeen were a bunch of dorks lost in a mindless "rock and roll fantasy" world where moronic cover bands play Scorpions to a handful of slack-jawed, white trash stoners. We were the only band [from the area] to make a large impact on a global level. Needless to say, the local music scenesters hated the Melvins. Fortunately for me, the rest of the world isn't as stupid.[30]

By Osborne's definition, Kurt was not stupid. Kurt worshipped the band, attending loads of practices and shows. In addition to influencing Kurt directly, Osborne also introduced him to popular punk bands like Black

Flag. Getting better at his guitar, Kurt once auditioned to become a member of the Melvins but was so nervous he did not make it. Kurt was not discouraged. He had discovered a whole new world of music and found something he was really interested in. After years of searching, he had finally found a world where he fit in.

Never one to mince words, Osborne later claimed responsibility for his role in defining the career of Kurt's future band, Nirvana. He said, "Nirvana changed the shape of music all over the world. And if it wasn't for the Melvins, they never would have existed. Remember: No Melvins, no Nirvana."[31]

Without discovering the Melvins, it is difficult to imagine where Kurt would have ended up. He was behind in his classes and had been kicked out of, or voluntarily left, most places he had lived. His relatives were fed up with his antisocial behavior. He lived with friends and sometimes slept in abandoned buildings. He told many people he even slept under a bridge near his mother's house. Years later, Kurt's bridge story became legendary when he wrote a gloomy song about it called "Something in the Way."

Several people who knew him well during that time dispute Kurt's version of the story. The small bridge crosses the Wishkah River and the muddy river's banks rise and fall with the tides of the Pacific Ocean. Even the river's name implies how horrible it would be to sleep there; "Wishkah" is the Indian word for "stinking water." Sleeping under the bridge would have been

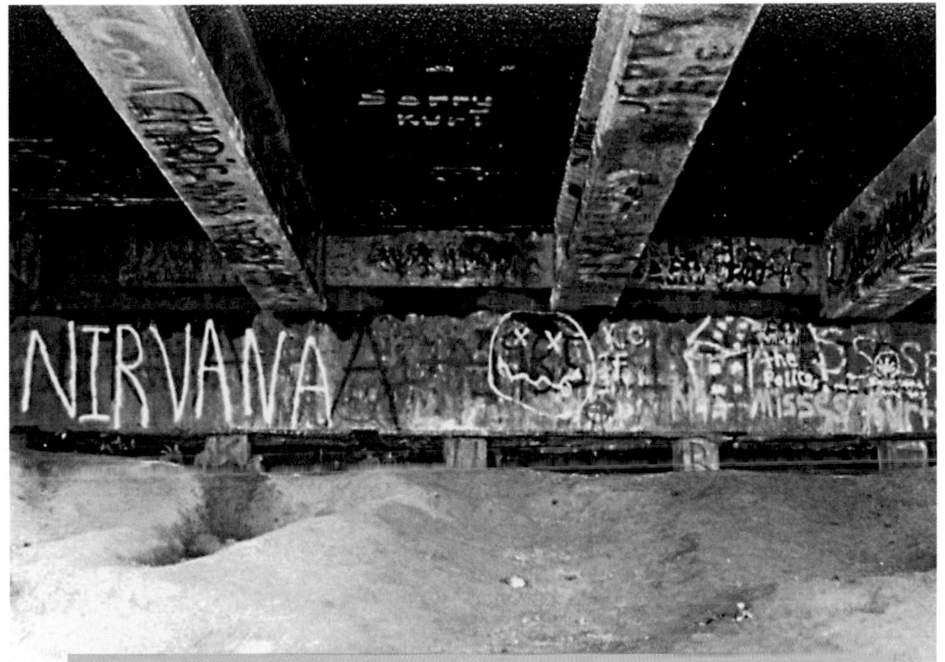

This is the bridge that Cobain was known to frequent. He also wrote the song "Something in the Way" about it. Today, fans have written messages to Cobain under the bridge.

possible but most who knew Kurt doubted he spent the night there. They say he did likely spend some time there because his mother had remarried, and Kurt did not care for his new stepfather. Hanging out underneath the bridge would have provided Kurt with a nearby place to get away from home for a short while.

Kurt eventually moved back with his father in Montesano but did not stay long before leaving again. He then moved to an even smaller town called North River to live with his friend, Jesse Reed. Jesse's dad, Dave Reed, had asked Kurt's parents if it would be okay. The house was big but North River was not. The small town was almost like a village, with so few school-aged students that all the grades attended class in one tiny building.

Dave Reed was a member of The Beachcombers, a popular regional rock band in the 1960s, and was now very religious. Being a rebellious musician, he felt he could relate to Kurt. He said, "I was heavily involved in the church at the time and welcomed him in. He even went to youth group."[32] Religion did not solve Kurt's problems. He and Jesse still smoked marijuana and played loud music. Dave Reed remembered, "They were just getting stoned wacko. I wouldn't know if somebody was stoned. Don't ask me how a guy playing in a band that long can be naive and not know someone was doing that, but I wasn't into it so I didn't know."[33]

Now seventeen, Kurt lived with the Reeds for nearly a year and occasionally attended church with the family. There was a lot of musical equipment in the house and Kurt used it constantly. Dave Reed said, "I had an old Sunn bass amplifier with a Carvin head and Kurt had a guitar. I let him use that stuff and he'd play on it for hours. It didn't seem like there was any rhyme or reason to his [chord] changes."[34] Thinking it would help him in the music business, Kurt also asked Dave Reed to introduce him to Stan Foreman. Foreman, also a member of The Beachcombers, was a promoter for Capitol Records in Seattle. The two did finally meet years later, after Kurt had become famous on his own. During that meeting, the tables had turned. Foreman jokingly asked Kurt to do him a favor: rerecord one of The

Beachcombers' songs. The remake would have certainly sold well and Foreman would have made a lot of royalty money for having written it.

Even the patient Reeds could not get Kurt back on a traditional path. He dropped out of high school and was asked to move out in 1985, shortly after his eighteenth birthday. Without a home, Kurt Cobain was again sleeping wherever he could. Soon, he and Jesse Reed got an apartment in Aberdeen, and Cobain got a job as a janitor at Aberdeen High School. Instead of attending classes at the school as he should have been, he was working there as a dropout. He did not keep the job long. For a period of time, Cobain also worked at the local YMCA as a lifeguard, janitor, and all-around activities coordinator for kids.

When Jesse Reed moved out of their apartment to join the military, Cobain was evicted for not paying his bills and was homeless again. During this period, he also had a run-in with the law. One evening, he was caught by a policeman spray-painting the words "Ain't got no how watchamacallit" on the side of a bank in downtown Aberdeen. Cobain was taken to the police station and fingerprinted. He was eventually released and ordered to pay a $180 fine.

Cobain soon moved in with LaMont and Barbara Shillinger's family. Two of the couple's sons, Steve and Eric, were close to Cobain's age and into the same type of music. LaMont Shillinger remembers first meeting Cobain, saying, "One evening about 7:30, Steve and

Eric asked if their friend Kurt could spend the night on our hide-a-bed as he wasn't getting along well with his step-father and didn't want to go back that evening."[35] The Shillingers said it was okay. The sons went outside to get Cobain. LaMont Shillinger, a conservative schoolteacher, said they brought in "this skinny, unkempt kid in pretty ragged clothes."[36]

Cobain spent the night in his own sleeping bag on the couch/hide-a-bed in the living room. Then, he stayed another night. Then another. Soon, he was a permanent fixture in the Shillinger house, doing chores and housesitting for the family when they went on an overnight holiday trip.

Cobain often did not have a job but was not the type to sit around doing nothing. LaMont Shillinger remembered, "He was always doing something like sketching, or painting, or designing album covers, or writing song lyrics or music."[37] Cobain and the Shillinger sons also played music in the garage and attended Melvins' practices, held just one block away. Cobain eventually left the house for good after he and Eric Shillinger got into a fight one day. Many different reasons have been given for the fight. Whatever the truth was, LaMont Shillinger was forgiving and invited Cobain back into the home. Though he had lived with them nearly a year, Cobain never returned.

Buzz Osborne is probably correct in saying the Melvins were heavily responsible for Cobain's career. Osborne introduced Cobain to different styles of music he would eventually grow to love and pattern his own songs after. In 1986, Cobain also recorded an important demo cassette with Osbornes's bandmate. Used frequently by musicians, demos are often sent to record labels or clubs as a way to show what the band sounds like. Cobain and Melvins' drummer Dale Crover went to Cobain's aunt's house and recorded several songs on her equipment, calling the material *Fecal Matter*. The tape included an early recording of the song "Downer," which was later rerecorded for Nirvana's first album. The *Fecal Matter* tape has never been released in its entirety but is heavily sought after by collectors. It is unknown how many copies exist but several people have claimed to have one.

Osborne was also indirectly responsible for Cobain meeting another important figure in his life. Krist Novoselic was also a Melvins fan who attended many of the band's practices and a lot of the same concerts as Cobain. Through this connection, the two met, and Cobain gave Novoselic a copy of his *Fecal Matter* recording. Novoselic, an outgoing Aberdonian, liked what he heard and the two formed a band. With the short Cobain singing and playing guitar and the extremely tall Novoselic playing bass guitar, the odd-looking duo rehearsed with various drummers before settling with Aaron Burckhard. Cobain was now sharing a house in Aberdeen with Melvins' bass player Matt Lukin. Though the house was dreadfully small and rundown, Cobain,

Novoselic, and Burckhard had a place to consistently practice—and party.

Chatty Ryan Aigner attended a majority of those practices. Aigner knew Novoselic's girlfriend, Shelli Dilley, and the couple had even lived with Aigner in Arizona, where he had moved after graduating high school. While they were there, Aigner helped Novoselic get a job as a painter. All three eventually moved back to Aberdeen and remained close friends.

Aigner remembered:

> In very short order, the world had changed and Krist had this band. Kurt had called him up and said, "We need to put a band together." I was very dedicated to what they were doing and showered them with praise. I'd already decided the stuff that Kurt was doing was far and above anything I'd heard from sort of a grass-roots level. I was, at that level, blown away.[38]

Aigner often told Cobain he thought the band was good enough to be on the radio, and Cobain scoffed every time it was mentioned. Aigner finally suggested the band break from the constant practicing and play a live show. The band agreed. One night, Aigner borrowed a van from his boss. The van having been backed up to the front door, everyone loaded up the equipment and took off. Aigner said, "Had Kurt known where he was going, he'd have never gone."[39]

Chapter 3

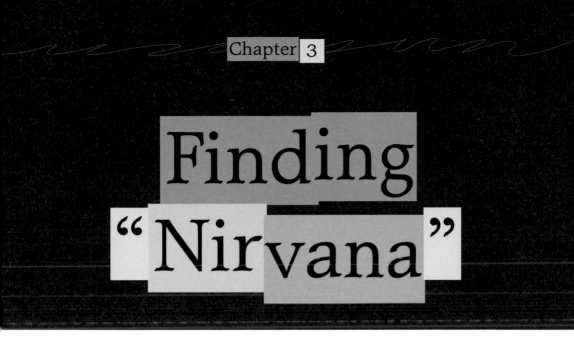

Finding "Nirvana"

As Cobain grew into his teens, the local logging industry had slipped from its heyday, and Aberdeen and Hoquiam's economies began slowing down. Having once lived in one of the richest areas on the West Coast of the United States, some residents were now moving away to find family-wage jobs.

Moving from Aberdeen had long been a common goal for teens. For reasons ranging from small-town boredom to lack of job opportunities, kids frequently talked of leaving as soon as they finished high school. Bigger cities like Seattle and Olympia were mentioned as places to go. None of the thrill-seeking teens mentioned Raymond, a much smaller town twenty-five miles to the south. But that is where Cobain and his band headed for their first show.

Further from Seattle, Raymond's geographic isolation and blue-collar populace offered less culture than Aberdeen. Cobain often complained about not being able to find suitable records in Aberdeen's music stores. Raymond did not even *have* a music store. Yet it was a house party in Raymond where Cobain's still unnamed band played its first show on March 7, 1987, two weeks after his twentieth birthday.

Aigner backed his work van up to the door at 17 Nussbaum Road and helped unload equipment into the corner of the living room. The room was already set up like a cheap recording studio because the men living there, Tony Poukkula and Jeff Franks, were in a band. Live music was played there all the time so it was normal for a band to come and play. With Cobain on guitar, singing into a microphone taped to its stand, Novoselic on bass, and Burckhard playing Franks' drum set, the Aberdeen band began its set.

The twenty people present were mostly there to party and certainly not there to see a band they had never heard of. So Cobain's band played eight songs to a mostly empty room, except for Cobain's girlfriend, Novoselic's girlfriend, and Aigner. Aigner later said:

> When the band was playing, they were really loud and really noisy and they weren't playing anything anyone had ever heard before. The rest of the people were through this doorway in the kitchen area where the sound was a little more tolerable. People would come over and look through the door[way]. They were listening to the music but there wasn't any big "Wow!" or anything.[1]

The regulars at the house party had never seen a band play like Cobain's. The partygoers were mostly into the popular hard rock songs of the day and what the Aberdeen band was playing was nothing like those. By request, they did play a crude version of Led Zeppelin's "Heartbreaker," but the rest of their songs were originals and far raunchier. It was obvious they did not fit in with the people there. Aigner remembered, "The camps didn't really blend well. None of these people knew Kurt or Krist, except Tony. Everyone else from Raymond was like, 'What is this freak show?'"[2]

Cobain said later, "We were really drunk, and we had some fake Halloween blood and we smeared it all over ourselves and played our seven [original] songs . . . And we alienated the entire crowd. The entire party moved into the kitchen and left the band, just left us there in the front room playing our songs."[3] When the band finished playing, Aigner picked up a guitar and jammed with Novoselic, then with the two guys who lived there. Cobain had gone outside to hang out, where Aigner later found him talking to a girl. He said, "Kurt was going on and on about these obscenities. The gal left and I looked over at Kurt and asked, 'What was all that about?' He said she had asked [for] the lyrics to 'Hairspray Queen.'"[4] When Aigner reminded Cobain that the curse words he was saying to her were not the lyrics, Cobain replied, "I know that," and walked away.[5]

The band and its group continued clowning around and making fun of the regulars. Tensions between the two groups grew and someone soon told Aigner that they should probably leave. Three hours after they arrived, Cobain and the gang packed up the van and drove home. That night, Cobain was more than 130 miles away from the big-city music scene in Seattle he longed to be part of. There was a lot of work to do before that could happen. Finishing the Raymond show, and surviving it, was an important first step.

The band still had not settled on a permanent name one month later when they played live on the radio. Calling themselves Skid Row (not to be confused with the then-upcoming New Jersey heavy metal band of the same name), Cobain, Novoselic, and Burckhard performed several songs on Olympia's KAOS, The Evergreen State College radio station. The band recorded the show for a demo, including a cover of the Shocking Blue song, "Love Buzz," and many of Cobain's originals like "Floyd the Barber," "Mexican Seafood," "Downer," and more. The recording helped the band get shows in established venues, like GESSCO Hall in Olympia and the Community World Theatre in Tacoma.

In early 1988, the band played a show at the Community World Theatre with the Melvins' Crover again filling in on drums. By that time, Burckhard had been let go from the band because he lived in Aberdeen and Cobain had just moved fifty miles away to Olympia. After falling behind on rent on the Aberdeen house he shared with Lukin, Cobain moved there to live with his girlfriend, Tracy Marander. The couple shared a small studio apartment, where the living room, kitchen, and bedroom are usually all in one room, with a separate, small bathroom. Cobain told one biographer the apartment was the size of a "shoe box."[6]

Cobain had met Marander a couple of years earlier. She was a year older and like a mother figure to him. Marander was also his main source of income and paid most of the bills for their apartment. Cobain did have a couple of odd jobs in Olympia but, just like his jobs in Aberdeen, they never lasted long. He mostly slept in, watched television, and played guitar, but Marander did not mind—at first.

Meanwhile, Novoselic had moved from Aberdeen to Tacoma with his girlfriend. Tacoma was twenty-five miles farther from Aberdeen than Olympia. Cobain and Novoselic liked to practice a lot, but making practices was hard for Burckhard. So he was out of the band.

During this period, Cobain's health became an issue. He was having severe pains in his stomach. He said, "You can feel it throbbing like you have a heart in your stomach and it just hurts really bad."[7] He visited several doctors though none seemed to be able to solve his problem. Eventually, he tried to self-medicate with illegal drugs, like heroin, which comes from the opium poppy plant and is very addictive. Cobain said he enjoyed using it because he felt it was the only cure he could find for his stomach pains. He said, "It started with three days in a row of doing heroin and I don't have a stomach pain. That was such a relief."[8] Kurt also admitted that he did heroin because he liked the way it made him feel. (However, heroin is a dangerous illegal drug that no one should ever try. It is very addictive and people who use it often die of overdoses.)

The band was no longer calling itself Skid Row by the time of the Community World Theatre show with Crover. They were now called Ted Ed Fred. Crover played with Cobain and Novoselic again the next day when they traveled back to Aberdeen to record a live video in a Radio Shack store.

Earlier in the day of the Ted Ed Fred show, Cobain, Novoselic, and Crover spent a few hours at Reciprocal Studios in Seattle. There, they recorded ten songs in five hours with producer Jack Endino. Endino was known for his work with some of Seattle's popular underground bands like Soundgarden and Green River and was also in a well-known band called Skin Yard. As most musicians were, he was also a fan of Crover's monstrous drumming. Endino remembered, "When Kurt called me and said, 'Yeah, my name's Kurt and I've got Dale from the Melvins helping me on drums,' I figured it must be all right because Dale wouldn't be in some [bad] band."[9]

Legend has it Endino's first impression was that the band members looked more like auto mechanics than musicians. He does not remember saying that but admits he might have. The songs Cobain's band recorded with Endino included "Downer," "Floyd the Barber," and "Paper Cuts." The last song they recorded was called "Pen Cap Chew," but it was not completely recorded because the band ran out of tape and did not want to pay for any more. Endino added, "They didn't have

Soon after gaining some experience playing shows, Nirvana was in the recording studio. One of the tools used in a recording studio is called a mixing board.

time to record more anyway," but they were very well rehearsed.[10] It is a good thing they were. They had to be in Tacoma in time for the concert later that evening.

Cobain sent the recording—nicknamed "The Dale Demo"—to several independent record labels with hopes of getting his band a contract. But it was Endino's generosity that ended up helping land the band a record deal. Endino said, "I liked the material a lot, that's why I kept a copy of it. I begged them to let me keep a copy of the tape just so I could let people hear it because I thought it was really cool. I thought I'd give it to a couple of friends of mine."[11]

Endino gave one copy to his girlfriend, Dawn Anderson, a writer for the small fanzine, *Backlash*. She eventually wrote a favorable article about the demo. It was the first article ever published on Cobain's band. Endino also shared the demo with his friends at nearby Sub Pop Records, a small, independent label run by Bruce Pavitt and Jonathan Poneman. Sub Pop had started out as a small magazine and was now in its beginning stages as a record company. Poneman heard the first song off the demo, "If You Must," and said, "The first time I heard that I just went, 'Ohhhhh my God.'"[12] Endino said he did not pass off tapes often. He said, "It was not common practice. I thought (the tape) was killer."[13]

Endino also shared the recording with a local college radio station called KCMU, which played "Floyd the Barber."

A Permanent Name

With all this happening, the band was still without a name and a full-time drummer, since Crover was still in the Melvins and only a temporary replacement. For a period, Dave Foster from Aberdeen drummed with Cobain and Novoselic. Foster played a few shows, including two major firsts for the band: Their first show in Seattle, on April 24, 1988, and their first under the name Nirvana. "Nirvana" means a state of complete happiness or a place, or condition of great peace or bliss.[14] Playing rock music was what made Cobain happy, so the name seemed appropriate. The name was also appropriate because the word "nirvana" was repeated fourteen times in "Paper Cuts." After several months of name changes, the band finally had one that stuck.

Nirvana did not perform well at their first Seattle show, held at a small club called the Vogue. Cobain was so nervous he threw up outside before it began.[15] The show was played on a "Sub Pop Sunday," a night sponsored by the record label. In a way, it was an audition for the band. After the show, most of the small crowd left disappointed with the band's performance. Cobain was hard on himself after the show and offered an excuse. He told an interviewer, "We felt like we were being judged; it was like everyone should've had scorecards. Plus I was sick. I puked that day."[16]

Fortunately, Sub Pop did not lose confidence in Nirvana. The label agreed to release a single from the band. It was a cover song, one written by one band and rerecorded by another. The song was "Love Buzz," originally done in the late 1960s by the Dutch group Shocking Blue. Foster was not in Nirvana when the agreement was reached. He had been fired. Cobain explained the reason in an unsent letter. He wrote, ". . . you are from a totally different culture. Our hobbies and interests are different, and a band can't be a unit unless all the members are compatible."[17]

"Our hobbies and interests are different, and a band can't be a unit unless all the members are compatible."

Foster was not really from a totally different culture. Just like Cobain and Novoselic, he was from Aberdeen, but Cobain now fancied himself as part of Olympia's more cultured scene and wanted to distance himself from his Aberdeen roots.

Chad Channing, who lived closer and seemed a better musical fit, had quietly replaced Foster. Channing first met Nirvana when they were playing at the Community World Theatre in Tacoma. At that time, Cobain and Novoselic's band was called Bliss. Channing said, "I liked what they were doing. I could tell there was something special going on."[18] Channing was short but his drums were gigantic and oddly shaped. They looked like they were from another planet.

After only a few rehearsals and just two shows together with Channing, Nirvana went back to Reciprocal Studios to record "Love Buzz" and three other songs. Endino said, "At first I didn't think [the material] was as good, because Chad was not as good as Dale on the older stuff. But then I saw that the direction was changing. The material was similar but not quite so edgy and noisy. It was getting a little more like classic '70s rock, not so punk."[19]

In November of 1988, "Love Buzz" was finished. The song was released as one side of a 45, a two-sided vinyl record with a song on each side. They were called 45s because they spun on the record player at forty-five revolutions per minute. Usually one song, the A-side, is the one a band thinks the radio will play and people will like most. The song on the other side is called the B-side. The B-side of the "Love Buzz" 45 was an original, "Big Cheese." Cobain was unhappy that the 45 was not made available in stores and that Nirvana was not being paid for it. It was only available to people who joined Sub Pop's "Singles Club." Still, one thousand copies were pressed and distributed.

Years later, the 45 became a collectible and people tried to make counterfeit copies of it. One way to distinguish an original from a fake was the writing on the album itself. The original one thousand had the words "Why Don't You Trade Those Guitars For Shovels?" etched into them. The phrase was something Novoselic's dad had once said. Eventually, after the band made it big, counterfeiters even copied that, and other means had to be used to determine authenticity.

The college radio station that first played "Floyd the

Barber" began playing "Love Buzz." Cobain was excited about this and wanted to hear himself on the radio. He listened for a while but "Love Buzz" never played. So when he and Tracy Marander were driving from Seattle to Olympia, Cobain made her stop the car so he could call the station to request the song. Shortly after, it came over the radio. Cobain was overwhelmed, saying, "It was amazing . . . (It was) morc than I ever wanted. But once I got the taste of it . . . I thought I would definitely like to hear my future recordings on the radio."[20]

Sub Pop soon agreed to release a full Nirvana album. Cobain was on his way to realizing his childhood dream of becoming a "superstar musician."

Chapter 4

Grunge Rock

As Nirvana's credibility slowly grew, Seattle's music scene continued gaining worldwide attention. Many of the city's bands Cobain had heard through his ties with the Melvins were now his peers. Soundgarden had released a couple of EPs (extended plays) with Sub Pop. Green River, including future members of two of the most popular Seattle bands ever, Pearl Jam and Mudhoney, were also releasing albums for the label. Sub Pop was signing a lot of bands, photographing them in the same style, and marketing them almost as if they were interchangeable. The young label was all about having fun. Record producer Steve Fisk said, "That's why all the bands wanted to sign to Sub Pop, because it looked like fun on the outside."[1]

Seattle, and Washington State in general, had made its mark on the national music scene in the late 1950s to mid-1960s, when the city's most popular bands were garage rock groups like The Wailers and The Sonics.

Garage rock is so named because it is thought a lot of those types of rough-edged bands could be found practicing in garages. It is a raw, yet emotional, type of music featuring basic guitar, bass, and drum parts. It is also a musical style full of tremendous energy.

When garage rock fell out of favor near the end of the 1960s, guitarist Jimi Hendrix picked up the Seattle torch, becoming an international superstar for four years before dying of a drug overdose in 1970. From there, various bands kept Seattle in the national spotlight, including hard rock acts like Heart and, later, heavy metal groups like Queensrÿche. Those bands achieved major fame throughout the world but they were not part of scenes unique to Seattle.

Though decades had passed and there was no direct lineage between garage rock and Nirvana, there were many similarities in style. Sub Pop and other regional independent record companies were signing bands playing a different type of music than was popular in the mainstream. The style featured the fast, basic tempos of garage rock music (which had morphed into punk rock in the 1970s), mixed with the loud, distorted guitars of heavy metal. Yet, underneath all the noise and sometimes hard-to-understand words, the songs themselves were melodic, memorable, and energetic.

The media began to call the Seattle bands' sludgy sound "grunge." No one is sure where the term came from.

The media began to call the Seattle bands' sludgy sound "grunge." No one is sure where the term came from. Many have credited Green River and Mudhoney singer Mark Arm for being the first one to use it in an interview. Arm does not think he was first, saying, "It's a line of [bull] that people keep repeating."[2]

Literally, the word grunge means dirty, messy, and unpleasant in any way. That was a pretty good description of what the music sounded like, but people were not finding it unpleasant. It was becoming popular and Nirvana was a big reason why. Though Nirvana's music did fit into the general grunge category, it differed in one major way from most Seattle bands of the time. Cobain's songs were a lot more poetic and catchy. He had a gift for writing pop songs. For that reason, Nirvana's music had the potential to appeal to a lot more people.

A Homecoming Show

With a successful single under its belt, Nirvana continued playing and practicing. On December 21, 1988, they even returned to Hoquiam for a show at the Eagles Hall. Though they had been named Nirvana for a while, the band again played under the name Ted Ed Fred. It was an important homecoming for twenty-one-year-old Cobain and twenty-three-year-old Novoselic. It allowed their families and fellow Melvins' followers a chance to see how the band had matured in the short time they had been away. They played fourteen songs in front of about sixty people. Novoselic played a majority of the concert without his shirt on, later stripping to just his underwear. Cobain wore a heavy flannel shirt with his long blonde hair tied back in a ponytail and tucked underneath a stocking cap.

They may have had music on the radio in Seattle and a record label behind them, but Nirvana was not the band most came to see. A local speed metal band called Attica had that honor. Coincidentally, Aaron Burckhard was now that band's drummer, and his new band was more popular than his old one, at least in Hoquiam and Aberdeen.

Attica was why Robb Bates, an upcoming local music promoter, was at the show. The only thing he knew about Nirvana was that Cobain was somehow associated with the Melvins. Still, he found himself near the stage, banging his head with Nirvana's music. He remembered, "Their stage appearance was good. Kurt was always moving around so he put on a pretty good show."[3] Bates said he became a fan that night and later traveled to shows in Olympia and Seattle to watch them. He said, "Nirvana started getting their name out and playing a lot of shows and their songs were sounding different. They were a lot more tight."[4]

After Nirvana played at Hoquiam, a small group of people who had traveled the fifty-five miles from Olympia to see them left their spots in front of the stage. They were replaced by dozens of others who had been sitting off to the side, patiently waiting for their local favorites to play.

Early Nirvana shows held elsewhere did not sell out but those fans that did attend were wild. They would jump up and down the entire time and bob their heads while slam dancing. The band would even let people jump on stage and leap off into the crowd below. Cobain would often join them. Stage diving had been taking place at punk rock shows for years, the theory being that the crowd would catch you when you jumped and let you down safely. That did not always happen and the potential for serious injury was great. Caught up in the moment of a wild rock concert, many people did not seem to care.

Nirvana was just as energetic as those who came to see them. Cobain's screaming vocals rarely let up, while Novoselic and Channing bounced and rocked out to the beat of their instruments.

With Channing on board and Sub Pop behind them, Nirvana began performing more frequently in Olympia, Tacoma, Seattle, and beyond. They got really worked up during shows and had a lot of aggression. At the end of many shows, Cobain would beat his guitar against other equipment and Novoselic would throw his bass. Channing's drums would get knocked over, sometimes from a guitar, other times from Cobain diving into them. Soon, audiences became disappointed if Nirvana did not break their instruments when the show was done. Since there was no money to replace their equipment every time, band members would just repair it as best they could before the next show.

After the Hoquiam show, Nirvana returned to Seattle to begin recording its first album with Endino. The recording agreement with Sub Pop was unique and not a good thing from the band's perspective. Nirvana had to pay for its time in the recording studio. Most record labels front the money and recover the recording costs from future record sales. But Sub Pop was just beginning and was not financially secure. The band did not have the money, either, so Cobain borrowed it from one of Channing's friends, guitarist Jason Everman. Everman later joined the band for a short time as its second guitarist but did not play on the album. Even so, a grateful Cobain listed him as a band member on the recording when it was finally released.

Nirvana recorded several songs at Reciprocal at a cost of slightly more than six hundred dollars. Some of the songs on the yet-unnamed album had been written years ago and some, like "About A Girl," were new. "About A Girl" was written about Cobain's girlfriend, Tracy Marander. It summed up what their relationship was like at the time he wrote it. Its simple melody was reminiscent of many of the Beatles songs Kurt had grown up listening and singing to. The mellowness of the song was a lot different from most of the heavier songs he had written. It showed Kurt had a talent for writing melodic pop songs. Endino said "About a Girl" was a "pleasant surprise" and Channing's drumming had improved greatly since their last session together.[5]

An early lineup of Nirvana poses in June 1989. From front to back are: Kurt Cobain, Jason Everman, Chad Channing, and Krist Novoselic.

The producer also saw growth from Cobain and Novoselic, saying:

> The first few times I saw them [live], they weren't very good. Kurt hadn't really figured out how to sing and play [guitar] at the same time. So his voice wasn't as good live as it was in the studio because he had to try and play the guitar parts. He figured out the key was to write simpler guitar parts so he could sing better.[6]

Nirvana also recorded a song called "School" with Endino, which was about the Seattle music scene. The scene's cliques reminded Cobain of his days at Aberdeen High School, where everyone seemed to need to belong to a certain social group. He explained to one reporter, "you grow up, having to deal with exactly the same things with your friends at parties and in clubs as you did in high school. It's exactly the same."[7] The song had just fifteen words, sung over and over. The two-word chorus featured Cobain howling, "No recess." These songs became part of the band's album *Bleach*, named after the bleaching process drug-users used to sterilize their needles to stop the spread of diseases. It was recorded over several different sessions.

". . . you grow up, having to deal with exactly the same things with your friends at parties and in clubs as you did in high school."

After they finished recording, Nirvana picked up the frequency of its live shows and Everman was brought on as a second guitarist to help Cobain with the guitar parts. The band toured clubs and bars in Seattle, Portland, San Francisco, Los Angeles, Houston, Chicago, Philadelphia, and more. Although *Bleach*—featuring a cover photo taken by Cobain's girlfriend—had been released to the public, it had not caught on so there were not many people at the first shows. As the tour wore on, more and more college radio stations began playing Nirvana's songs and more people came to see them live. Channing said, "We noticed a significant difference in the people that were showing up to the venues. Everywhere we were playing was packed."[8]

Prior to the release of *Bleach*, the band was making just enough money to eat and pay for gas for their van to get to the next show. They would spend nights wherever they could, whether with friends, acquaintances, or in the van. As more people began to attend shows, the band received more money but was still always broke.

Everman was fired after a show in New York City on July 18, 1989. There were two weeks left of the tour, but Nirvana canceled the remaining shows. Some believe Cobain fired Everman because his posing and flamboyant, hair-whipping style made the band look like a hair metal band, which was something they did not want to be. Another reason given was that Cobain and Novoselic did not get along with him, though Channing did. Cobain explained, "We kicked him out 'cause he didn't like to do the songs that we like. He wants to play slow, heavy grunge and we want to write pop songs."[9]

Almost immediately, Everman joined Soundgarden for a short stint as its bass player. The remaining members—Cobain, Novoselic, and Channing—were getting along well. Channing said, "Our relationship was really pretty fun. We never got under each others' skins because we were always too quiet."[10]

"We kicked him out 'cause he didn't like to do the songs that we like."

Some small but powerful magazines and newspapers began writing stories about Nirvana and publishing reviews of *Bleach*. Most of them were favorable. Although the band was not from Seattle and did not even live there, they were grouped as part of the "Seattle sound," along with bands like Mudhoney, Soundgarden, and others. The influential *CMJ New Music Report* said "'Nirvana' could become the coolest thing since toast."[11]

In addition to citing Everman, although he never played on the album, *Bleach*'s credits featured two other noteworthy points. The first being Novoselic's first name was spelled "Chris," the spelling he used throughout most of his childhood. In 1992, he changed it back to the original Croatian spelling of "Krist." His parents were from Croatia and he had spent some time there growing up. The second was Cobain's name, which was spelled "Kurdt Kobain." Some say he had changed the spelling of his first name to mimic another popular Aberdeen musician, Kurdt Vanderhoof of the band Metal Church. Though Metal Church was, at the time, far more successful than Nirvana, getting Cobain to admit to copying the guitarist for a heavy metal band would not have been easy. Cobain's own explanation to one biographer is more punk rock and somewhat sad. He said, "I think I wanted to be anonymous at first. . . . I wish nobody ever knew what my real name was. So I could some day be a normal citizen again."[12]

Touring Abroad

Nirvana began its first overseas tour in October of 1989. They co-headlined with another Sub Pop band, Tad, and the tour began in Newcastle, England. By this time, many media outlets in that country were hyping the Seattle sound. England's *Melody Maker*, one of the oldest music magazines in the world, was behind Nirvana. So was John Peel, a legendary disc jockey for BBC Radio. Nirvana played its first session on Peel's popular show during this tour. More media coverage generally means more popularity and more people coming to see a band when they are in town. Nirvana's reputation continued to grow while visiting The Netherlands, Germany, Austria, Hungary, Switzerland, Italy, France, and Belgium. The tour was long and grueling and the band continued to smash their equipment at many stops along the way.

Humor was also common in the band's shows. At the show in Linz, Austria, Novoselic screamed the wrong words to "Scoff" while Cobain fixed his guitar mid-song. After the song, Cobain resumed working on his guitar while Novoselic stepped up to the microphone and talked about how much fun he was having in "Australia," intentionally messing up the country's name. He then mentioned he was disappointed he had not seen any kangaroos. There were no kangaroos in Austria. As those who understood English shouted obscenities at the band, Cobain flipped his long hair out of his eyes, looked at Novoselic, and smiled. Laughing, Novoselic stepped across the stage to take a sip of beer before playing the opening notes to "Love Buzz." Cobain and Channing joined in and the show continued. Cobain had his own fun with the crowd that night, repeatedly telling them to "pogo." The crowd did not need his reminder. They were already doing it, hopping up and down in small groups and slamming into each other.

The long tour took a mental and physical toll on Cobain. During a show in Rome near the end of the tour, he climbed onto the top of a stack of speakers above the stage and threatened to jump. Sub Pop's Jonathan Poneman said it was because Cobain's guitar had been malfunctioning and he was fed up with it. Poneman said, "If it didn't kill him, it would have injured some people below him and he was serious about it."[13] Poneman promised to buy Cobain a new guitar and bought him a train ticket to the next tour stop so he could relax alone and did not have to ride in the crowded van with the rest of the guys.

The band finished the tour and returned back home to rest and close out the year. The biggest highlight of the last few days of 1989 was Novoselic's wedding to his longtime girlfriend, Shelli Dilley. It took place in the couple's Tacoma apartment. Cobain was not the best man. Instead, the honor went to Cobain's former Aberdeen roommate, Matt Lukin, who had left the Melvins and was now a member of Mudhoney.

Nirvana continued writing new songs and performing. They started 1990 with a show at the University of Washington in Seattle, where they destroyed so much equipment at the end, they were banned from playing there again.[14] After a few more dates in the Pacific Northwest, Nirvana played a short tour with Tad through San Francisco, Los Angeles, Mexico, and Phoenix. Touring constantly is one method new bands use to get themselves in the public eye, sell merchandise like T-shirts and music, and hopefully at least break even financially while doing it. Touring was fun but it was the rehearsals Nirvana felt most important. They were working on songs Cobain was writing for the next Nirvana album.

They destroyed so much equipment . . . they were banned from playing there again.

In April, Nirvana went into a studio in Madison, Wisconsin to work with producer Butch Vig, who later became the drummer for a popular 1990s band called Garbage. Nirvana was there to record some ideas for songs for its second album. They stayed long enough to record seven songs, including "In Bloom," "Lithium," and "Polly."

Cobain wrote "Polly" about a 1987 crime where a girl had been abducted after a punk rock show at the

Kurt Cobain smashes his guitar during a 1990 concert.

Community World Theatre in Tacoma. Nirvana had played there several times, so the crime hit close to home with Cobain. The girl was raped and tortured by her abductor before she escaped. Cobain believed the crime was twisted and wrote the song from the perspective of the abductor. As "Polly" proved, Cobain had a soft spot for those he felt had been victimized, especially women, minorities, and homosexuals.

While in Wisconsin, Nirvana booked a show in nearby Chicago at the Cabaret Metro. Greg Kot, the pop music critic for the *Chicago Tribune*, went to the show to see another band but ended up being blown away by Nirvana's opening set. He said, "I don't remember much about the songs; it was more Cobain's voice, the graininess of it, the ferocity of the delivery. He'd play his guitar and throw himself around the stage as if in the jaws of some giant, unseen Rottweiler. For the finale, he threw himself headlong into the drum kit and destroyed his guitar. I stood there, slackjawed, six feet away from him, and held up a hand to stop the runaway bass drum from rolling on top of me. I had no idea if these guys were any good or not; I still didn't hear the songs through all the racket they threw up. But I knew I'd never forget this performance."[15] Many people reported similar first experiences at Nirvana shows. The band was always wild, reckless, and unpredictable.

The recording stop in Wisconsin was sandwiched between several Midwest and East Coast tour dates, including a show in New York City where many crowd members were record company representatives and musicians. People were becoming curious and word-of-mouth was spreading about Nirvana.

The band was gaining steam, but everything was not perfect in Cobain's world. Two big breakups were looming. He called Tracy Marander from the tour and told her he did not want to live with her anymore. It was never officially stated but, after three years, the couple had broken up. Cobain continued to live with her after he returned from touring, but Marander eventually moved out.

Cobain soon started dating another Olympia woman named Tobi Vail. Vail was also a musician and later started a band with Kathleen Hanna called Bikini Kill. Vail was part of Olympia's "riot grrrl" movement, a subculture of empowered female punk rockers. Her empowerment carried over into her relationships, as well, and Vail was not as interested in commitment as Cobain was. They acted so much like friends; many didn't know they were dating.[16]

On the band front, Cobain and Novoselic grew weary of Channing's drumming. Cobain had played drums off and on since the days of beating on pans in his grandparents' home near Montesano and often criticized Channing's playing. Channing, meanwhile, was not happy with his role in the band. He wanted to help write more songs but Cobain and Novoselic were not allowing him to. Whether Channing was fired or not

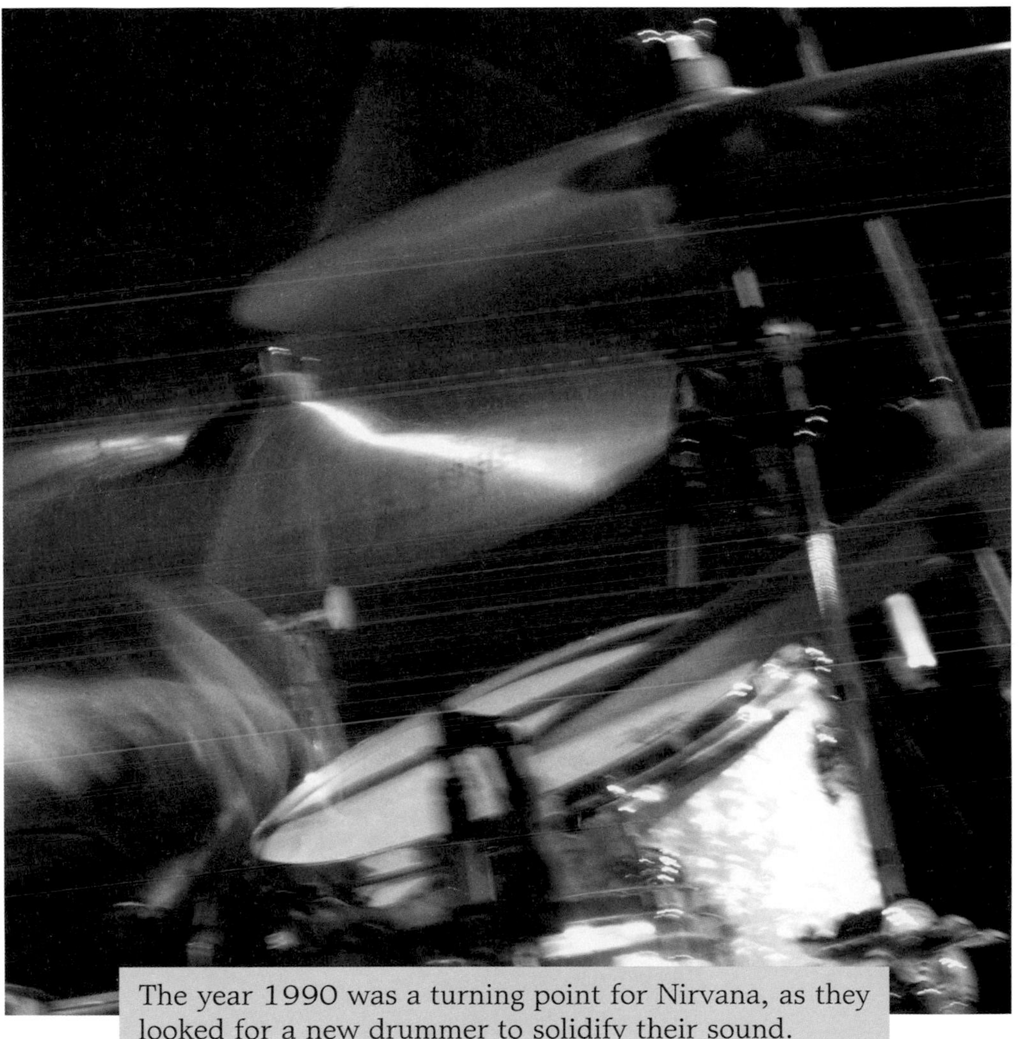

The year 1990 was a turning point for Nirvana, as they looked for a new drummer to solidify their sound.

was never resolved. One side said he was and one side said he left on his own. Whatever happened, Nirvana was again without a drummer. The Melvins' Dale Crover came back to drum with the band for a short summer tour of the West Coast. For one show in Seattle, Mudhoney's Dan Peters played drums with Nirvana. For different reasons, neither was a permanent solution.

The success of *Bleach* and subsequent touring had drawn the interest of several major record labels, which wanted to lure Nirvana away from Sub Pop. Meanwhile, Cobain and Novoselic were in the same position they were in two years earlier. They were searching for a record label and without a drummer.

Chapter 5

Smells Like Success

Nirvana's connection with the Melvins again helped them find a band member. This time the Melvins did not lend their own drummer, but told Cobain and Novoselic about a punk rock drummer from Washington, D.C., named Dave Grohl.

Grohl was in a band called Scream when he learned of Nirvana's opening. He said, "I talked to Buzz Osborne from the Melvins and he told me, 'I think Nirvana might call you because they need a drummer.' They didn't call, so I called them."[1] Grohl was in Los Angeles on a break from touring with his band, which was having personnel issues of its own. He went to Seattle and auditioned with Cobain and Novoselic. The trio clicked almost immediately. Grohl remembered, "They wanted a drummer that played really big drums and hit extremely hard, so things worked out from there."[2] Grohl was definitely a hard hitter. He often hit the drums so hard that they—or the sticks—would break. He had patterned his style after drummers in popular hard rock bands, like John Bonham of Led Zeppelin, Phil Taylor of Motörhead, and Keith Moon of the Who.

Grohl was also helpful to the band because he could sing well. Adding a backup vocalist to sing with Cobain made the band sound better live and in the studio. Grohl moved to Tacoma to live with Novoselic and his wife and the band began to practice and learn the songs Cobain had already written. Grohl was a quick learner and the missing piece the band had been looking for to take its sound to the next level. Novoselic said, "Once Dave joined, Nirvana was just like a tight machine. It just all fell into place."[3]

Three weeks after Grohl joined, the trio played its first show together. Only two weeks after that, they went to the United Kingdom on a weeklong tour, where Cobain told one reporter, "I don't wanna have any other kind of job, I can't work among people. I may as well try and make a career out of this. All my life my dream has been to be a big rock star."[4]

"All my life my dream has been to be a big rock star."

For several reasons, the band was not happy with Sub Pop and continued taking offers from major record labels. It signified an important shift in thinking for Cobain. He often said he would never sign to a major label. Strange as it sounds, those on independent labels like Sub Pop often look down upon the big record companies. The belief is that bands signing with major labels become puppets and are not allowed to play what they want anymore. Instead, they are thought to have to play the type of music the labels think will make money. It is called "selling out."

However, being on a major label does have many advantages and Cobain found one especially pleasing. One of his biggest problems with Sub Pop was that Nirvana's albums were not found in many stores. In cities in which the band was touring, people were complaining that they could not find *Bleach*, and it annoyed Cobain. He wanted as many people as possible to hear his music. Distribution deals are what get records into stores and Sub Pop's distribution deal was inadequate. Major labels' distribution deals are much better and their records are available in most every store that sells music. Cobain found that very appealing.

Through their friends in the band Sonic Youth, Nirvana found one major label they thought would allow them to be themselves *and* get their music into stores. Nirvana had toured with Sonic Youth, who were signed to the DGC label, part of Geffen Records. Sonic Youth played a style of music similar to Nirvana's and were happy with Geffen. Though more than a half-dozen major labels were looking to sign Nirvana to a contract—including MCA, Columbia, and Capitol—Nirvana eventually chose Geffen. The contract was for a $287,000 advance plus several favorable creative and financial options. Some of those trying to sign Nirvana wanted to pay them more but Nirvana went with the one they thought would most let them be themselves.

Before signing the band, Geffen had to buy Nirvana out of its contract with Sub Pop. Sub Pop received $75,000, a percentage of all of Nirvana's album sales, and the rights to release one last Nirvana song. The song, "Molly's Lips," was a cover of a song by the English band, The Vaselines. The two-person Vaselines were one of Cobain's favorites. Later, he got a chance to sing "Molly's Lips" in concert with them.

Meanwhile, Grohl had moved from Novoselic's house into Cobain's apartment in Olympia. Cobain had lived there by himself since he and Marander had broken up. The musicians' apartment was always filthy. Cobain said, "It was the most filthy pigsty I'd ever lived in."[5] Almost every day, the two drove the thirty minutes to Tacoma to practice with Novoselic for hours. Novoselic remembered, "We were very disciplined and we took rehearsals and playing music seriously. There was really no messing around."[6]

Though the band was going better than ever, Cobain was depressed. He wanted a long-term relationship and Vail was not looking for that. The couple, that many did not even know was dating, broke up.

Geffen had paid Nirvana a lot of money but they had not seen much of it after all the fees were taken out, including the seventy-five thousand dollars owed to Sub Pop. Cobain's new management company allowed him to have one thousand dollars a month.[7]

Depressed, nearly broke, and insecure, Cobain began taking heroin again. His ex-girlfriend, Tracy Marander, witnessed at least one such episode. Prior to attending a concert one night, she heard a crash in the bathroom of Cobain's apartment. She rushed in to find Cobain with his sleeve rolled up (heroin is often injected in the arm), and drug paraphernalia all around him. Marander told a biographer, "I don't think he did it when we were going out, as far as I know."[8] In addition to relieving his stomach pain, the introverted Cobain felt the drug took him out of his shell. Marander said, "He felt like he could go out and have a good time and talk to people and not feel uncomfortable."[9] She found Cobain's drug use ironic because he had a fear of needles and was even afraid to get his blood drawn.[10]

Depressed, nearly broke, and insecure, Cobain began taking heroin again.

Scenes like that were still infrequent and the band continued practicing, playing shows, and recording. Their first studio session with Grohl was on New Year's Day, 1991, at Music Source Studios in Seattle. They recorded six songs, with titles like "Aneurysm" and "On a Plain."

A Defining Moment

One of the most important moments in Nirvana history took place on April 17 in Seattle, when the band was playing a show at the O.K. Hotel. Nearly finished with their nineteen-song set, they debuted a new tune.

The song was called "Smells Like Teen Spirit." It was a reference to Cobain's ex-girlfriend, Tobi Vail. Vail's friend, Kathleen Hanna, had once written, "Kurt smells like Teen Spirit" on the wall of Cobain's Olympia apartment, referring to the brand of deodorant that Vail wore. Hanna was simply saying Cobain smelled like Vail. Cobain took the sentence and wrote a song about it. He did not know Teen Spirit was a deodorant. The song he wrote was about social groups and trying to fit in at events, like parties. The theme was similar to the earlier song, "School," where Cobain had screamed "no recess" over and over. This one, however, had more than fifteen words.

When a big event happens in people's lives, they generally remember where they were when it occurred. The people in the crowd at the O.K. Hotel were in that situation. Though none of them had heard the song before, they later remembered every detail about it. Sub Pop's Jonathan Poneman was there. He said, "I remember going, 'Wow, God this is a really good song.' Then it comes to the chorus and everyone went, 'Oh, my God, this is one of the greatest choruses of any song I've ever heard in my life.'"[11]

The song was a little more than five minutes long and began with a simple guitar part similar to "Louie, Louie," which Cobain had played as a teen. It also featured soft-loud dynamics, meaning the song would alternate between quiet verses and near-deafening roars on the chorus. It was a pattern many of Nirvana's songs

Producer Jerry Dennon holds a gold record for the Kingsmen's 1960s hit song "Louie, Louie." Dennon helped contribute to the garage-rock "Northwest sound," which later influenced Kurt Cobain. "Smells Like Teen Spirit" had the promise of being Cobain's first gold record.

would follow. Just like "Louie, Louie," many of the words to "Smells Like Teen Spirit" were mumbled and hard to understand. Still, it was an instant success with the crowd at the O.K. Hotel. The more people heard it, the more the song's popularity grew.

Later that month, the band drove to Los Angeles to begin recording their album with producer Vig. They wanted to work with him because they felt comfortable with him the last time they worked together. The studio was not glamorous and was in a suburb just outside the big city. Cobain called his dad and told him how well his band was doing and that they were going to record their first major label record. Father and son had not talked for a long time and spent an hour filling each other in on their lives.[12]

Finding "Love"

The band spent about a month working and recording the album, living in apartments while doing so. It was not all work and no play. Though Cobain would not know it for a while, his quest for a long-term romantic relationship was about to be fulfilled. Backstage at a concert, he ran into a bleach-blonde woman named Courtney Love. They had met before and she had even sent him some gifts, including a heart-shaped box with various items inside. Love was well known on the independent music scene. She had acted in a couple of movies, traveled the world, and was the singer and guitarist in a band called Hole. She had also been a member of early versions of the band Faith No More and played in Babes in Toyland with Kat Bjelland and with both Bjelland and Jennifer Finch in an early band called Sugar Baby Doll.

Love's father was an acquaintance of the popular 1960s band The Grateful Dead and her mother was a homemaker. Though Love was almost three years older than Cobain, the two had a lot in common. Like Cobain, she spent her early years around musicians and was from a broken home. Love's parents divorced when she was five. Her mother also remarried and had more children with her new husband. Then her mother and stepfather divorced, and her mother remarried again. All this happened before Love was eight. They both also did drugs and played guitar and sang in rock and roll bands. When Cobain and Love met backstage in Los Angeles, Hole's first album, Pretty on the Inside, was just about to be released.

Backstage at a concert, he ran into a bleach-blonde woman named Courtney Love.

By June 1991, Nirvana's album was finished but it still did not have a name. The band finally settled on *Nevermind*. The word suggested apathy and was also a lyric from "Smells Like Teen Spirit."

For the album cover, the band used a photograph they had taken of a four-month-old baby boy swimming underwater. The baby was naked, causing many controversies. At first, the record label did not want to use the photo but finally agreed. One photo on the inside of the album showed Cobain holding up his middle finger to the camera. In the band's biography, written by Geffen's publicity department, Cobain was quoted as saying, "Maybe we can change some kid's life and stop him from becoming a welder or a sleazy lawyer."[13]

"Smells Like Teen Spirit" was the first song on the album. It was also chosen as the first single to be released on radio and was sent to stations at the end of August. The single went on sale to the public a couple of weeks later. Even after the reaction the first time it was played live, it was not an immediate smash. The record company did not expect it to be, thinking the hit song off the album would be "Lithium."

"Maybe we can change some kid's life and stop him from becoming a welder or a sleazy lawyer."

The band filmed a music video for "Teen Spirit" anyway. The video was set in a high school gym. It was patterned after one of Cobain's favorite movies, *Over the Edge*, a story about teenage rebellion. As Nirvana played on a basketball court, tattooed cheerleaders, dressed in tight black tank tops, danced for the crowd. The tank tops had a red letter "A" on them, symbolizing anarchy. The shoot was exactly that. A crazed janitor was also in the cast, dancing around with a mop. Some say the placement of the janitor was an inside joke because Cobain had worked as a high school janitor.

Most of the extras were fans that had heard the band needed an audience. As the song played on, the crowd grew wilder, just as they would at a Nirvana concert. They began jumping up and down, off the bleachers, and slamming into each other. The video ends with Cobain breaking the neck off his guitar while the crowd destroys the rest of the band's equipment. Unlike most productions, the set destruction was not rehearsed. Though Nirvana had been destroying their instruments for years, the "Smells Like Teen Spirit" video presented a whole new energy to MTV viewers when it was aired on the network. The punk rock craziness of Nirvana was something most people had never seen and the video was vital to Nirvana's career. It was also vital to MTV's success, because it helped the station appeal to a new set of viewers who had grown tired of MTV's mainstream music choices.

Before the album was released in the United States, Nirvana left for a short tour in Europe with Sonic Youth and a band called Dinosaur Jr. The three bands played several shows together but the most talked about was the annual Reading Festival in England. Part of Nirvana's performance there was later included in the documentary film, *1991: The Year Punk Broke*. At the end of their set, Cobain threw himself into Grohl's drums and dislocated his shoulder.[14]

Back in Seattle on September 13, Nirvana held its album release party for *Nevermind*. It was not a concert, just a time where several people got together to talk and be among the first to listen to the new record. Nirvana was not happy with that boring scene, so they started a food fight. The band was kicked out of its own party. Three days later, Nirvana played an in-store show at Beehive Records in Seattle. With all the breakable merchandise around, in-store shows were usually calm affairs. With Nirvana, nothing was normal. The band was supposed to play a few songs but ended up playing thirteen. Dozens of fans were allowed into the store while just as many watched from the outside.

Four days later, Nirvana left on a North American tour to support *Nevermind*. The tour began in Toronto, Canada. The Melvins, the band Cobain and Novoselic idolized a few years earlier in Aberdeen, were now the opening act for shows Nirvana was headlining. The tour made its way across the country and included stops in most major cities. In Chicago, Cobain met Courtney Love again and the two officially began dating.

In the parking lot afterward, the bouncer, back from the hospital, punched the window out of the cab Nirvana was in, attempting to get at Cobain.

In Dallas, the stage was so small and the crowd so full that the bouncers were the only thing separating the crowd and band. The human barrier was not good enough. As his band played "Love Buzz," Cobain dove over the bouncers and into the crowd with his guitar. As one bulky bouncer tried to pull him back, Cobain intentionally slammed him in the head with his guitar, causing him to bleed. The bouncer punched Cobain and the music stopped, with Grohl, Novoselic, and others trying to subdue the angry bouncer. The bouncer was taken to the hospital and Nirvana finished the show. In the parking lot afterward, the bouncer, back from the hospital, punched the window out of the cab Nirvana was in, attempting to get at Cobain. The cab sped off and the band was safe.

While Nirvana was away on tour, "Smells Like Teen Spirit" found its way onto the *Billboard* magazine charts. The charts are one of the main ways used to measure the success of songs and albums. *Nevermind* was released in stores on September 24 and debuted at No. 144. MTV first aired the "Smells Like Teen Spirit" video in September and put it into heavy rotation in October. That helped push *Nevermind* to Gold status, meaning it had sold five hundred thousand copies. Most bands would have been happy if that was all they ever sold. Geffen said they would have been happy if the album had sold fifty thousand copies. *Nevermind* had already sold ten times that amount. It was only the start of things to come.

Nirvana mania began popping up everywhere. More and more people started coming to their shows. Cobain and Novoselic even made an appearance on the popular MTV show, *Headbanger's Ball*. The show featured music videos from heavy metal bands. Nirvana was not a heavy metal band but was invited as a guest anyway. Cobain decided to poke fun at the situation, which was similar to the one in Raymond, where he had to entertain people who liked a different type of music than he played. Cobain showed up wearing a woman's yellow gown. He said he did it because he thought he was going to a ball.

When Nirvana's North American tour ended on Halloween in Seattle, the concert had to be shifted to a larger venue due to high demand for tickets. The clubs originally booked to hold Nirvana's shows were no longer large enough. People were buying *Nevermind* in droves and trying to decipher the lyrics. The words were not printed inside the album, so no one knew for sure what Cobain was singing. Many interpretations were way wrong. In the middle of 1992, everyone finally found out what Cobain was saying when the single for "Lithium" was released. It included lyrics for every song on *Nevermind*.

Word of Nirvana's accomplishments extended back to the non-MTV viewers in Aberdeen when Cobain's mom wrote a letter to the editor of the local newspaper. It was directed to parents of kids wanting to spend time playing music rather than doing homework—exactly what had gotten Cobain removed from guitar lessons years earlier. His mom said she had just gotten off the phone with her son and he told her *Nevermind* had just gone Platinum, meaning it had sold one million copies. She wrote, "The hours and hours and hours of practice have paid off."[15] Later, Cobain's mother said, "if you happen to read this, we are so proud of you and you are truly one of the nicest sons a mother could have."[16] She ended by telling Cobain to make sure he brushed his teeth and ate his vegetables.[17] His mother had not seen

Cobain jumps in the air during a 1992 concert in England.

him in some time at this point. It had been even longer since Cobain had seen his father.

When the letter was published on November 21, 1991, Nirvana was in the middle of a European tour lasting the rest of the year and into 1992. That trip featured several highlights, including a defiant stop on England's popular *Top of the Pops* TV show. The *Top of the Pops* producers wanted Cobain to lip-sync and he refused. He was finally allowed to sing live to a prerecorded song and he sang the words drolly, in a deep voice. Novoselic and Grohl made it obvious they were not playing their instruments, but the show went on. It was another example of how little Nirvana cared what others thought. They were on the verge of becoming the biggest band in the world—breaking rules and making their own.

Chapter 6

Dethroning the King

A Michael Jackson album was at the top of the *Billboard* charts when 1992 began. Those preferring rock music over Jackson's dance pop were mainly listening to what was called "hair bands," mostly male-fronted metal bands with long, pouffy hair coated with sticky hairspray. Those bands were an updated twist on 1970s-era glam rock. They often wore makeup and their looks were usually as important as their music. With grunge music, everything changed. The music was now becoming the main thing that mattered, at least to the bands. There were no wardrobe consultants or costume changes between songs.

On stage, Cobain wore the same clothes he wore around the house and often slept in them, too. It may sound disgusting to most but it was the essence of grunge music. It was everything popular music of the time was not. Many felt it was more real and pure, what they believed music was supposed to be. Similar-sounding

Seattle bands like Pearl Jam, Soundgarden, and Alice In Chains (which had, at one time, been a hair band) began getting a lot more attention from MTV and the radio. Newspapers were publishing big stories and magazines were putting them on their covers. All three had signed major label contracts before Nirvana but did not reach superstardom until after Nirvana paved their way.

Michael Jackson may have been known as the "King of Pop," but his days on top of the charts were coming to an end. *Nevermind* went double platinum in January 1992. Nirvana had sold two million albums and were preparing for a big TV appearance that would help them sell even more.

Live from New York

Performing on the NBC show *Saturday Night Live* (*SNL*) is considered a big success for bands. Nirvana appeared on the show on January 11. They played "Smells Like Teen Spirit" and "Territorial Pissings" and ended by trashing their instruments. Perhaps to purposely upset any homophobic viewers or simply to rebel, Cobain and Novoselic French-kissed on camera as the credits rolled.

Earlier that day, *Nevermind* hit No. 1 on the *Billboard* charts. Established artists like Garth Brooks, U2, Metallica, Guns N' Roses, and even Michael Jackson, were selling less than Nirvana. The album also went to No. 1 in several other countries. Once *Nevermind* hit the top of the charts, the strategy of many in the music business changed. Nirvana's type of music was being called "alternative rock," meaning anything not currently played on popular radio. Nirvana's success gave dozens of other alternative rock bands, like Los Angeles' Stone Temple Pilots and Chicago's Smashing Pumpkins, the opportunity to be played on the radio and MTV. Many stations across the country even changed their formats and *only* played alternative music. Several similar-sounding bands also followed Nirvana onto the charts and some even changed their sound to try and mimic Nirvana. Soon after *Nevermind* hit No. 1, alternative rock was what everyone was listening to. Strangely, it was still called alternative.

January 11 had been a great day for Cobain. His band's album was the most popular album in the United States and he had completed a successful performance in front of millions of viewers on live TV. But with Cobain, not much was as easy as it should be. He was not handling fame well. Partially because he could now afford it, he had begun using more heroin and was addicted to the drug. The morning after the *SNL* show, he overdosed and Love found him in a drug-induced coma.[1] Around the same time, Love became pregnant with Cobain's child. It was not a great situation for a child to be born into, so husband and wife vowed to stop using drugs so their child would be born healthy and into a drug-free environment.

Back in Aberdeen, Cobain and Novoselic's moms were interviewed for an article in the local newspaper. Cobain's mom, who had just returned from New York where she watched her son on *SNL*, said Cobain was amazed by all the exposure he was receiving in the media. She said he "can't believe how many places he sees himself."[2] She also theorized about the creation of Nirvana's songs, saying, "I think a lot of Kurt's songwriting comes from his pain in childhood."[3]

Ryan Aigner, who had set up Nirvana's first show nearly four years earlier, was not surprised when he first heard of Nirvana's mega success. Several times he had told the band he thought they had the talent to make it big. But he was "shocked and surprised because the rest of the world finally figured out what I had thought all along. That was the only surprising thing. I just thought I was vindicated."[4]

Nirvana left on another short tour to Australia, New Zealand, Japan, and Hawaii, where Cobain and Love got married on February 24, 1992. For the ceremony, Love wore a dress and Cobain wore his pajamas. Grohl was there but Cobain's longtime friend and bandmate Novoselic was not. The reason depends on who is asked. Love says she banned Novoselic's wife, Shelli, from the wedding. Shelli Novoselic says she objected to Cobain and Love doing drugs and chose not to go.[5] For most of his career, Cobain denied using hard drugs like heroin. He later admitted he had used frequently and gave his reason for lying. He said, "I had a responsibility to the kids [his fans] to not let on that I did drugs."[6]

Nevermind stayed hot, thanks in part to the release of "Come As You Are" as both a single and a video.

The naked baby on the cover of *Nevermind* may have been underwater but the guitars in "Come As You Are" sounded like they were played underwater. The swirling video footage also featured water effects, matching the sound perfectly. Once it became popular, "Come As You Are" caused a controversy when another band claimed Nirvana had stolen the guitar part from one of its songs. The band sued but eventually lost. It was not the only lawsuit Nirvana faced. A Christian band named Nirvana sued Cobain's Nirvana for using the name, arguing they had used it first. A little later, a second band named Nirvana, this one from England, filed a lawsuit over the use of the name. Nirvana paid settlements to each of the other two bands, the cases were dropped and Cobain, Novoselic, and Grohl continued to call their band Nirvana.

The third single and video from *Nevermind* was for "Lithium," the song the record label initially thought would be Nirvana's biggest hit. By this point, "Smells Like Teen Spirit" was such a huge smash, it was unlikely any song could top it. When "Lithium" was released, *Nevermind* had sold nearly four million copies and was still a hot seller. "Lithium" was not more popular than "Smells Like Teen Spirit," but was well received and helped maintain the album's momentum. The video was a combination of live performances and featured one scene with Novoselic carrying a feeble-looking Cobain on his shoulders while spinning 'round and 'round.

Other artists were noticing Nirvana's success and

gaining from it. "Weird" Al Yankovic released a song called "Smells Like Nirvana" that was a big hit. Yankovic was famous for his song parodies, where he took an artist's song and changed the lyrics to make them humorous. He was very successful at it and had won two Grammy Awards for his work. His videos were often played on MTV. "Smells Like Nirvana" was Yankovic's interpretation of "Smells Like Teen Spirit." It made fun of the fact that no one could understand what Cobain was singing in the song. Yankovic started off by singing, "What is this song all about?" and ended by screaming a bunch of random sounds. The video was shot in the same gym as Nirvana's and even used the same actor to play the janitor. Cobain, who had agreed to let Yankovic use his song, said he liked the parody.

The band soon took a back seat to Cobain's personal issues for a while. It was not the only time the band took a lengthy break. Grohl said later it was one of the most frustrating parts about being in Nirvana. "If I have one complaint about being in Nirvana, it's that we didn't play enough. Eight months would go by without any shows."[7]

Cobain and the still-pregnant Love rented an apartment in Los Angeles. Love's band, Hole, also signed a contract with Geffen Records. Now, both the husband and wife were signed to major labels. The initial advance in Hole's contract was worth even more money than Nirvana's. Many similar-sounding alternative rock bands were being signed to record contracts and since alternative music was now the popular craze, bands playing that style, like Hole, were worth more than they had been before Nirvana's breakout.

Shortly thereafter, even the Melvins were signed to a major label contract. Their music was much further removed from the mainstream than Nirvana's, Hole's, or most any other band's, for that matter. But the association with Nirvana was enough for Atlantic Records to take a chance. Cobain was even called on to help produce the Melvins' first Atlantic album, 1993's *Houdini*. In 1996, Atlantic dropped the Melvins from its roster because they were not selling enough albums. In the early nineties, that did not matter as much. Everyone was hoping they would be the one to discover the next Nirvana and were willing to take many chances to do so.

Spokesman for a Generation

Selling so many records also had a negative effect on Novoselic and Grohl. Because he had written most of the songs, Cobain decided he deserved a bigger share of the profits. Novoselic and Grohl were not happy but agreed to give them to him. Some believed Love was the reason Cobain was making this demand. Because of that and other reasons, the band was not getting along as well as before. Still, they managed to rehearse and do a short tour of Europe. Thousands were at every show.

Cobain was quickly becoming the representative for

an entire generation of people—Generation X. The term basically encompassed all who were teens in the 1980s and early 1990s. They were the generation after the Baby Boomers, the surge of Americans born right after World War II. Grunge music was Generation X's music. Gen-Xers were typically thought of as lazy, flannel-wearing slackers who were not living up to their potential. The media began calling Cobain the spokesperson for Generation X and "Smells Like Teen Spirit" became the anthem of the generation. Needless to say, Cobain did not like the media's labels. He adhered to a punk-rock philosophy. When something became mainstream, he no longer wanted to be part of it. Now his band was the mainstream. He may have said he wanted success when he was younger but now he had it and realized it was not as much fun as he thought it would be. So he rebelled.

At one photo shoot for *Rolling Stone* magazine, Cobain wore a homemade T-shirt with the words "Corporate Magazines Still Suck" on the front. Another time, he wore a shirt reading, "Grunge is Dead." Both were Cobain's way of saying he was not happy with being so heavily publicized and did not like the labels he had been branded with. He and Love soon got even more unwanted publicity when an article in *Vanity Fair* magazine came out. Love was pregnant when the article was written. In it, she was portrayed as doing all the things pregnant women are not supposed to do if they want to have a healthy baby. The writer said Love was smoking cigarettes. Most damaging was the claim that the mother-to-be had used heroin while pregnant.

The article came out one week before Love had her baby. On August 18, 1992, Frances Bean Cobain was born. The baby was named after singer/guitarist Frances McKee of The Vaselines. Her odd middle name was given to her because Cobain thought she looked like a bean in a previous sonogram. Although Frances Bean appeared healthy, people were outraged over the *Vanity Fair* article. They thought Cobain and Love were unfit parents. The courts ordered Frances Bean temporarily removed from her parents' custody. Cobain and Love were not allowed to be alone with their daughter. Eventually, Frances Bean was given back to them but not without much stress. The couple did interviews to help control the damage and had to submit to drug tests. Even though *Vanity Fair*'s accusations were never substantiated, the article damaged the couple's credibility.

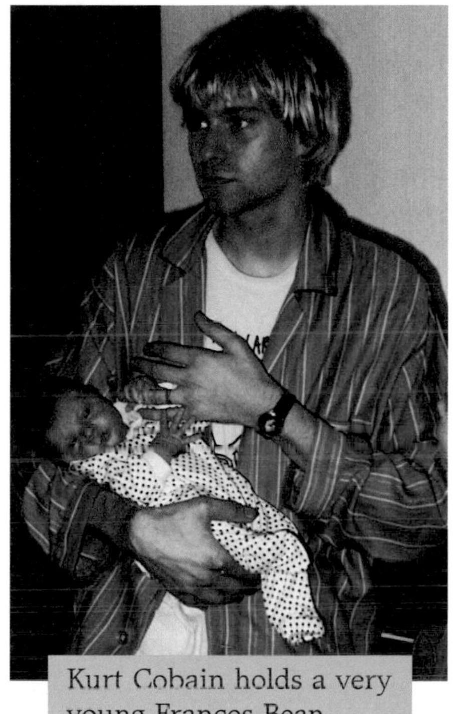
Kurt Cobain holds a very young Frances Bean.

While all this was happening in his personal life, Cobain was still the leader of the biggest band in the world and had many band obligations to deal with. Nirvana performed again at the Reading Festival in England. The first time they played there a year before they were just one band of several on the bill. This time, they were the headliner. Nirvana had so much pull in the music industry they even helped determine what other bands would play the show. Cobain never forgot his roots and always helped bring some of the lesser-known bands he liked into the public eye. The Melvins and Mudhoney were there. Some of the other acts included the Beastie Boys, Public Enemy, and Smashing Pumpkins.

In the days leading up to the show, rumors spread that Cobain was in bad health. He was not, but decided to play a joke on the crowd of sixty thousand. Cobain was pushed onto the stage in a wheelchair. Wearing a medical gown, he sang parts of the song "The Rose" in a weak voice before falling to the ground as if he had fainted or died. When he got up, he grabbed a guitar and launched into "Breed," then played twenty-four more songs for the wild crowd.

Cobain was pushed onto the stage in a wheelchair.

Nirvana's next performance was at the MTV Video Music Awards in Los Angeles, where they also won two awards. When "Smells Like Teen Spirit" won Best Alternative Video, the band sent a Michael Jackson impersonator on stage to accept the award as a joke. The band accepted the second award themselves, for Best New Artist.

MTV wanted Nirvana to perform "Smells Like Teen

Spirit" at the awards but settled for "Lithium," because the band did not want to play its biggest hit. Cobain had wanted to play a new song called "Rape Me," but MTV would not allow it. Yet when Nirvana began playing, Cobain strummed the first few bars of "Rape Me," frightening MTV's producers, who were about to pull the plug on the band. Cobain immediately shifted into "Lithium" and all were relieved.

Backstage, Cobain and Love got into an argument with Axl Rose, singer for the band Guns N' Roses. Rose had been among those who had talked bad about Cobain and Love's drug use. After Nirvana played "Lithium," Grohl jumped off his drum kit, ran up to the microphone, and said, "Hi, Axl." Before that, Cobain threw his guitar and toppled a speaker, while Novoselic staggered off stage injured. He had thrown his bass into the air and tried to catch it, but it hit him on the head instead, knocking him down.

The day after the MTV awards, Nirvana played a benefit concert in Portland, Oregon, to help raise money to fight a proposed law limiting the rights of gays. Cobain had always believed in equal rights for gay people. In the liner notes of a future album, he wrote, "At this point, I have a request for our fans. If any of you in any way hate homosexuals, people of different color, or women, please do this one favor for us—leave us alone. Don't come to our shows and don't buy our records." The words came from *Incesticide*, which was released in December 1992. It was a collection of rare songs Nirvana previously recorded, including an accelerated version of "Polly." The album cover featured Cobain's painting of a baby holding onto a skeleton and two red poppies, Cobain's favorite flower and also the one from which heroin is made. *Incesticide* showed many new fans that Nirvana did indeed get their success from the ground up. Since most people had not heard of Nirvana prior to *Nevermind*, many thought they were an overnight success. The early music on *Incesticide* showed they had been at it for a while. One video was eventually released from the album. It was for the song "Sliver" and featured scenes of a young Frances Bean dancing to the music. The toddler was not really dancing. Cobain was holding her up and moving her to the music with his arms hidden from the camera's view.

Despite the controversies surrounding Nirvana, or perhaps because of them, *Nevermind* continued to sell well. A fourth video from the album was released in November for "In Bloom." It showed the three band members clean-cut and dressed in suits. The video was shot to look like the band was appearing on the old-time TV program, *The Ed Sullivan Show*, the program where the Beatles—fronted by one of Cobain's idols, John Lennon—had made their live debut in the United States. Scenes of Nirvana performing were spliced with scenes of girls in the crowd going crazy and screaming for the band, just as they had for the Beatles. Another version of "In Bloom" was shot, with Nirvana wearing dresses.

Nirvana at the beginning of 1993. From left to right are: Dave Grohl, Kurt Cobain, and Krist Novoselic.

Nirvana's influence was spreading beyond music. Cobain's choice of clothing—old T-shirts, ripped blue jeans, and flannel shirts from second-hand stores—became fashionable. Everyone wanted to dress like him. Cobain wore those types of clothes because that is what he could afford growing up, but kids now wanted to wear the style because Cobain was doing it. Rich kids were paying large amounts of money for designer flannel shirts and expensive, preripped jeans. Magazines were devoting large amounts of space to Cobain's way of dress. Kids began keeping their hair unwashed and stringy, like Cobain's. Grunge was no longer just a musical term but a fashion style as well.

When the nominees for the 1992 Grammy Awards were announced in January 1993, "Smells Like Teen Spirit" was nominated for Best Hard Rock Performance with Vocal. The Grammy Awards are considered the biggest awards given out in the music business. Songs from two other Seattle bands, Alice In Chains and Pearl Jam, were also nominated in Nirvana's category, as well as one from Guns N' Roses. A fifth band, The Red Hot Chili Peppers, ended up winning.

Though he had become rock music's biggest star, Cobain did not ignore where he was from. He, Love, and Frances Bean made several trips back to Aberdeen and Montesano to visit relatives. Cobain's grandpa Leland Cobain remembered, "Every time he came back from one of those tours, didn't matter what time of the day or night it was, he'd wake us up and come in. We'd

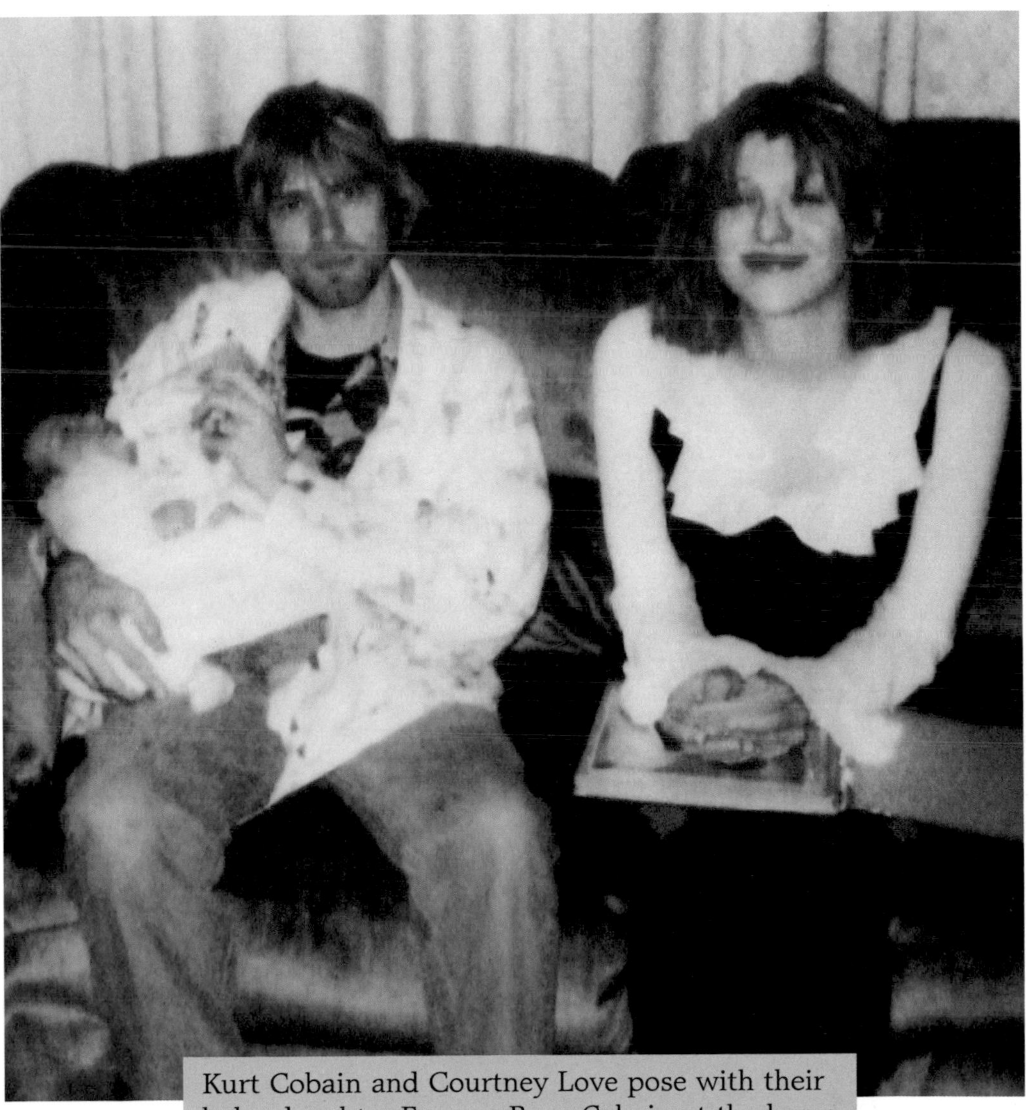

Kurt Cobain and Courtney Love pose with their baby daughter Frances Bean Cobain at the home of Kurt's grandfather, Leland Cobain.

always find something for him to eat—a couple of old pieces of pizza or something. He'd sit on the floor by (his grandmother's) bed and talk to her."[8] A photo from one such visit shows Cobain and Love sitting on the couch, with Cobain holding his daughter in his arms and feeding her from a bottle. Although he had said for years he wanted to be a rock star, many people think Cobain wanted to return to the simple, small-town life permanently. Nirvana's ex-drummer Chad Channing said years later he believed, "Things for Kurt got tougher and tougher. All of a sudden you find out that so much of your life you've got so little control of. I can't ever imagine Kurt being happy as a pawn in anybody's game. I don't think he was the kind of person to enjoy the kind of success that he had."[9]

"Things for Kurt got tougher and tougher."

Chapter 7

Bored and Old

As Nirvana grew from a band into a cultural phenomenon, Cobain continued to try to find ways to be himself and not sell out. When every magazine in the world would have loved an exclusive interview, he agreed to only speak to one, a magazine for gays called, *The Advocate*. The interview was published in February 1993. The handlers of Nirvana's publicity did not want Cobain to do the interview, so he set it up himself. In it, he talked about distaste for the band Guns N' Roses, mostly because he did not like their macho conduct and songs, and talked about homosexuality. He said, "I used to pretend I was gay to [mess] with people. I've had the reputation of being a homosexual every day since I was 14."[1]

Nirvana again defied their employers' wishes by going to a studio in Minnesota to record their new album. The entire album was recorded there in two weeks with producer Steve Albini and eventually called

In Utero. Cobain wanted to call it *I Hate Myself and Want to Die* but the record label did not like the idea. There was also supposed to be a song on the album by the same name, but it did not make the cut. It was released later, however, on a compilation for a TV series called *Beavis and Butt-head*.

Even without the bluntly titled "I Hate Myself and Want to Die," the songs on *In Utero* were not like the ones on *Nevermind*. Though still melodic, they were heavier rock songs and not as radio friendly. The lyrics were also more personal. Cobain wrote about several of his life experiences, including his estranged relationship with his father in the album's first song, "Serve the Servants."

Cobain's grandfather believes he knows what inspired Cobain to write the song. When Cobain brought a large bouquet of flowers to his sick grandmother in a hospital in Seattle, his dad called the room. Leland Cobain said his wife, "made Kurt talk to his dad because they were on the outs. I heard Kurt say he knew a lot of the stuff that had been said about his dad wasn't true and it was his mother that was saying it all. He said as soon as he got back from a tour, maybe they could get together again and talk things out."[2] After Kurt hung up the phone, he told his grandparents he

After Kurt hung up the phone, he told his grandparents he realized a lot of the bad stuff he had been told about his father was not true.

realized a lot of the bad stuff he had been told about his father was not true.

Like *Nevermind*'s "Polly," *In Utero* discussed the issue of rape. This time it was in "Rape Me," which Nirvana had wanted to play at the MTV awards. About the song, Cobain said, "This is my way of saying: 'Do it once, and you might get away with it. Do it a hundred times. But you're gonna get it in the end.'"[3] The song was said to have another meaning. Many say the song was also Cobain's way of saying the intrusive media kept "raping" him and would not leave him alone. Another song off the album, "Heart-Shaped Box," was a reference to the box and gifts Love had sent him before they started dating. The last song, "All Apologies," sounded very different from the first track. "Serve the Servants" had been full of loud, distorted guitars and pounding drums, but "All Apologies" was a melodic, quiet pop song.

Executives at Nirvana's record label were not happy when they first heard *In Utero*. They had expected an album similar to *Nevermind*, one with catchy songs people could sing along to. They especially wanted one that would be played on the radio and MTV, and would again sell several million copies. Cobain said, "I think the general consensus was that the album may not sell as much and they were concerned about that, but they never once put any pressure on us."[4]

Some say Cobain intentionally made the album less radio friendly to help escape some of the fame he was beginning to grow tired of. One of *In Utero*'s songs was even called "Radio Friendly Unit Shifter." Many thought this song was his way of saying he was fed up with stardom. Radio-friendly unit shifter is a term used in the record industry to describe an album or song that will be played on the radio and sell a lot of copies. Bowing slightly to the Geffen's wishes, Nirvana did agree to do a little more work on the album before it came out in stores. They eventually remixed "Heart-Shaped Box" and "All Apologies." Not surprisingly, both those songs were later released as singles.

When finished recording *In Utero*, Nirvana played its first show in three months on April 9, in San Francisco. It was a benefit for Bosnian rape victims and organized by Novoselic, who was becoming active in politics. The band began the concert with the obvious choice, "Rape Me," but did not play "Polly."

Police Calls

All the while, Cobain continued using heroin. On May 2, he came home from a party at a friend's house. He did not look good and went to his bedroom. By this time, Cobain and Love had moved back to Seattle and bought an expensive home in an upper-class neighborhood. The police were called and their report said when Love went in to check on him, Cobain was "shaking, became flushed, delirious and talked incoherently."[5] The report said he had "injected himself with $30–$40 worth of heroin . . . [and] this type of incident had happened before."[6] Cobain was taken to the hospital in an ambulance and fully recovered.

One month later, police were back at the house. This time Cobain was taken to jail. The police report said, "Kurt Cobain and (Courtney) had gotten into an argument over guns in the household. (Courtney) stated that she threw a glass of juice into Kurt's face and then Kurt pushed her in turn. (Courtney) pushed Kurt back, at which time Kurt pushed her to the floor and began choking her, leaving a scratch."[7] Cobain spent three hours in jail and posted $950 bail to get out. Police took three guns from the house. Cobain and Love both later told separate members of the press the police report was wrong. Domestic violence charges filed against Cobain were eventually dropped.

Cobain spent three hours in jail and posted $950 bail to get out. Police took three guns from the house.

Somehow, the band was still thriving. On September 2, Nirvana won another MTV Video Music Award. This time it was "In Bloom," for Best Alternative Video. On September 19, the video for "Heart-Shaped Box" premiered on MTV. Two days later, *In Utero* was released. Despite the record company's worries that it would not sell, it entered the *Billboard* charts at No. 1.

The big chain stores of Wal-Mart and Kmart decided not to sell the album. One reason was because the back cover had a collage of plastic fetuses, similar to the sperm-to-baby drawing Cobain had won an award for in high school. Another reason stores would not sell

Nirvana poses at MTV's Video Music Awards after they won a "moonman" for Best Alternative Video for "In Bloom." From left to right are: Krist Novoselic, Dave Grohl, Kurt Cobain, and the video's director, Kevin Kerslake.

In Utero was because of the song "Rape Me," even though the song was speaking out *against* the crime. Cobain faced a tough decision because he wanted the record to be available to all people who wanted it. For some retailers, the band agreed to change the artwork and the title of "Rape Me" to read "Waif Me." However, the song lyrics were never changed.

Many people called Cobain a sellout for altering the album so it could be in stores. Mark Kates was Nirvana's A&R, or artists and repertoire, representative at the time. As an A&R rep, Kates worked for Geffen and was the main link between Nirvana and the label. Kates did not believe Cobain was selling out, saying, "These were the only kind of stores that he could buy records in when he was a kid. It was a drag, but it was a bigger drag if people couldn't get the CD."[8]

For the first time since Jason Everman was fired four years earlier, Nirvana added a second guitarist to supplement its live shows. Again, the main reason was to help Cobain with the guitar parts so he could focus more on singing and entertaining the crowd. Pat Smear from the punk band The Germs was chosen to fill the role. Cobain said, "I want to be able to have eye contact with the people in the audience once in a while. So having another guitar player is a total relief."[9] The foursome's first performance together was a big one. It was back on *Saturday Night Live* on September 25. There, the band played "Heart-Shaped Box" and "Rape Me," the song that MTV had said they could not play on its cable network.

A Hometown Friend

Three weeks later, Nirvana left on a long U.S. tour promoting *In Utero*. In Kalamazoo, Michigan, the band realized how small the world was. At a photo shoot for *Rolling Stone* magazine, Cobain and Novoselic ran into another person from their small hometown of Aberdeen. Cyndy Warlow had once ridden the school bus with Cobain's uncle, Gary Cobain. She was hired by photographer Mark Seliger to be the wardrobe stylist for the session. Warlow put some thought into her clothing choices. She picked items she felt characterized Nirvana's career at that time.

Warlow had the company make Cobain a "Bobcats" cheerleader uniform with the inscription "Song Queen Kurt" sewn onto it.

First, she called Aberdeen High School and got the name of the company that made the school's cheerleading uniforms. Since Aberdeen High's nickname was the Bobcats, Warlow had the company make Cobain a "Bobcats" cheerleader uniform with the inscription "Song Queen Kurt" sewn onto it. Cobain even had pompoms. The wardrobe stylist said, "I always thought he was really in touch with his feminine side and would get a kick out of it. He was always feeling that he had to cheer everything along when I think he would have just liked to have escaped into the background."[10] She also clothed the band in leather outfits. She said it symbolized, "Kurt's feeling on the fact that most of his fan-base was homophobic."[11] For the cover photo,

Warlow dressed the band in expensive suits to show they were now a corporate band. Even though they said many times how they disliked it being that way, Nirvana was not only a band, it was also a big business whose income employed many people. The band got the jokes and played along with all the wardrobe selections. The suits shot was used on the cover of *Rolling Stone* in January 1994.

After the session, Warlow, Cobain, and Novoselic talked about growing up in Aberdeen. When the stylist got home, there was a phone message from Cobain thanking her for "really taking the time to think about him and what he was about instead of just trying to make a fashion statement."[12]

The tour took a break after the November 15 show in New York City so Nirvana could rehearse and perform on MTV's *Unplugged*. For *Unplugged*, bands went into a studio and played acoustically. Nirvana sounded quite different without all the amplifiers and big speakers they usually used. They rehearsed for two days and surprised everyone on the third day when they did the whole show in one take. Though bands would often play songs over and over again to get them right and then splice them together in editing, Nirvana did not have to do that.

With cello player Lori Goldston sitting in, Nirvana not only played its own songs but also some covers. They played a song by David Bowie called "The Man Who Sold the World" and a Vaselines song called "Jesus

Doesn't Want Me for a Sunbeam." Near the end, they invited some friends on stage. It was two members from the band Meat Puppets and the whole group played three of that band's songs. Novoselic also played some different instruments during the show, including the guitar and the accordion.

The last song of the night was a showstopper. It was a cover of an old blues song by Leadbelly called "Where Did You Sleep Last Night." At the end, Cobain put his all into one final scream before walking off stage. Love was not there to witness one of her husband's most shining moments. Cobain had banned her from attending. Producer Alex Coletti said, "Kurt didn't want her around, because he was nervous enough already."[13]

The *In Utero* tour resumed a week later in Florida, and continued into 1994. It featured three shows in Seattle, including one filmed for MTV's *Live and Loud* concert series. Though the show's name indicated it would be, it was not aired live. MTV showed it on New Year's Eve, although it was filmed in the middle of December. The tour's other two stops in Seattle were at the Seattle Center Arena on January 7 and 8, 1994. No one knew it at the time but they were the final two shows Nirvana would ever play in the United States.

Cobain continued growing tired of Nirvana being lumped into the grunge musical category. He hinted several times Nirvana would soon change musical directions. He thought they should try to play a different type of music. Many of their songs started out quietly, then progressed into a loud chorus. Cobain was growing tired of that style of songwriting. He told one journalist, "I don't know how long we can continue as Nirvana without a radical shift in direction . . . We're all tired of being labeled."[14]

He was also becoming more fed up with stardom. Everywhere he went, people were asking for his autograph and snapping photos. Sure, he had wanted Nirvana to sell a lot of records but he had no idea how great an impact doing so would have on his personal life. He told a reporter from *The New York Times*, "I'm not going to subject myself to being stuck in an apartment building for the next 10 years and being afraid to go outside of my house."[15]

"I'm not going to subject myself to being stuck in an apartment building for the next 10 years and being afraid to go outside of my house."

A False Report

The band went back to Europe in February and played seventeen sold-out shows in less than a month. The March 1 show in Munich, Germany was the last Nirvana show, although it was supposed to be just the middle of another tour. But on March 3 in Rome, Cobain again succumbed to drugs. Love had flown in from London to visit her husband and woke on March 4 to find Cobain in a coma on their hotel room floor. He had overdosed on the tranquilizer Rohypnol mixed with champagne and was holding a three-page suicide note in his hand.[16] Cobain was rushed to the hospital in an ambulance, where he recovered. Back in the United States, however, one news network inaccurately reported Cobain was dead. The false news of his death spread quickly and fans began to mourn.

Cobain was still alive and Love called his mother from Rome to tell her what was going on. The mom told *The (Aberdeen) Daily World*, "I took one look at my son's picture and saw his eyes and I lost it. I didn't want my son gone."[17] The news came at a bad time for Cobain's mom. She had recently survived a bout of breast cancer and was also going through a divorce with her second husband, Pat O'Connor.[18]

No one was taken to jail this time but the police took four guns, some ammunition, and a "bottle of assorted, unidentified pills."

Cobain stayed in the Rome hospital for four days before flying back to Seattle. The rest of the tour was canceled. Everyone was told the overdose was accidental and not to worry about Cobain. They said he was fine, but there was plenty to worry about. On March 18, the police were back at Kurt and Courtney's Seattle home. The police report said Cobain "had locked himself in a room and that he was going to kill himself. (Courtney) also stated that he had a gun in the room . . . (Kurt) continued to state that he is not suicidal and doesn't want to hurt himself."[19] No one was taken to jail this time but the police took four guns, some ammunition, and a "bottle of assorted, unidentified pills."[20] Cobain left the house.

Love, with Cobain's bandmates and friends, staged a drug intervention at the house on March 25. A drug intervention is where friends and family let the drug user know how much they care about him or her. They also talk about how the person's drug use affects them. The goal is for the user to see how messed up he or she is, get treatment, and quit using. During the intervention, Love threatened to leave her husband. Smear and Novoselic threatened to break up the band. No one wanted to do those things, but they all wanted Cobain to stop using heroin. The threats were merely their last resort.

They did not work on the stubborn Cobain. Love flew to Los Angeles to check herself into drug rehab, and Cobain stayed behind and continued using heroin. After several conversations with a psychiatrist, he finally agreed to fly to Los Angeles for treatment. Cobain entered treatment on March 30. Two days later, he climbed over a six-foot brick wall and fled the treatment center to fly back to Seattle.[21]

Love said Cobain called her on April 1 and said, "Just remember, no matter what, I love you."[22] It was the last time the couple ever spoke. On April 4, a missing person report was filed with the Seattle Police Department. Some say it was Cobain's mom who filed the report and some say it was Love who did it, in the mother's name. It said, "Mr. Cobain ran away from a

California facility and flew back to Seattle. He also bought a shotgun and may be suicidal."[23]

It seemed like the whole world was looking for Cobain. His face was on every TV station and in many magazines and newspapers. He was the most famous rock star in the world. Still, no one could find him.

Chapter 8

Joining a "Stupid Club"

Electrician Gary Smith arrived at Cobain's Seattle home on the morning of April 8, 1994, to spend the day installing a new security system. Walking by the room above the large home's garage, he glanced inside and saw a body lying on the floor. Smith said, "At first I thought it was a mannequin."[1] Just the day before, a private investigator had searched the home but did not notice the area above the garage.[2] The electrician had found Cobain, who had finally succeeded at doing what many said he had been trying to do for a long time. He had taken a large dose of heroin then shot and killed himself. There was a suicide note near his body, addressed to his imaginary childhood friend, Boddah.

Kurt Cobain was only twenty-seven years old.

Smith called his workplace on a two-way radio and someone there called the police and local radio station KXRX. Thinking it was a prank, the radio station hung up on the caller more than once. Eventually, disc jockey

Marty Riemer talked with the caller who said, "I have got the scoop of the century for you. You are going to owe me some Pink Floyd tickets for this one."[3] KXRX's producer eventually called the Seattle Police Department and learned a patrol car had been sent to Cobain's house. Less than fifteen minutes after the anonymous caller first dialed the station, Riemer went on the air to announce what he knew. He said, "Seattle police are responding to a call of a dead body at the home of Kurt Cobain. An eyewitness at the scene claims that the body is that of Cobain himself, victim of an apparent suicide."[4]

The station then called the Associated Press, which put out an alert across its news wire. Riemer still has that bulletin, which he tore off the printer when it came into his station a few minutes later. It read, "SEATTLE POLICE ARE INVESTIGATING A REPORT THAT A BODY HAS BEEN FOUND AT THE HOME OF NIRVANA SINGER KURT COBAIN."[5]

News spread quickly. Riemer remembered:

> The phones exploded. First from our audience, and then when the story hit the AP, calls began coming in from across the country and around the world. We weren't convinced ourselves that the body was Cobain's, so our first reaction in the studio was that we wanted to put the genie back in the bottle.[6]

About ten minutes after the announcement, Cobain's sister, Kim Cobain, called the station. Riemer did not know what to say to her. He told his receptionist, "Tell her all we know we reported on the air. And, if it's true, we're very sorry."[7] That type of outpouring of emotion and love for Cobain went on for days. It was a continuation of the support he had seen from fans while alive.

In Cobain's hometown of Aberdeen, newspaper reporter Doug Barker saw the bulletin come across the Associated Press wire about the same time Riemer had. Barker's young daughter had been a playmate of Kurt's half-sister and the reporter knew Cobain's mom. Nearing its daily deadline, the paper waited for more confirmation before acting. Barker said, "We didn't immediately scramble because it could have been a lot of different people. It (eventually) became pretty clear that it was Kurt. We knew we had to go talk to Wendy."[8]

Unsure whether he would have to break the news to Cobain's mom, Barker slowly drove the two miles to her house and knocked on the door. When a grieving aunt met Barker at the door, it became obvious the family had already heard. The reporter and Cobain's mom hugged and held each other near the doorway. Barker said, "She just sobbed and couldn't talk."[9] Eventually, she told the reporter about the detective that had been hired to locate Cobain. Barker said, "She'd sort of go in and out between anger and frenzy—utter, utter anguish. It was horrible to see. She kept rocking and saying, 'I don't know what to do. I don't know where to go. I don't know what to do. I don't know where to go.'"[10]

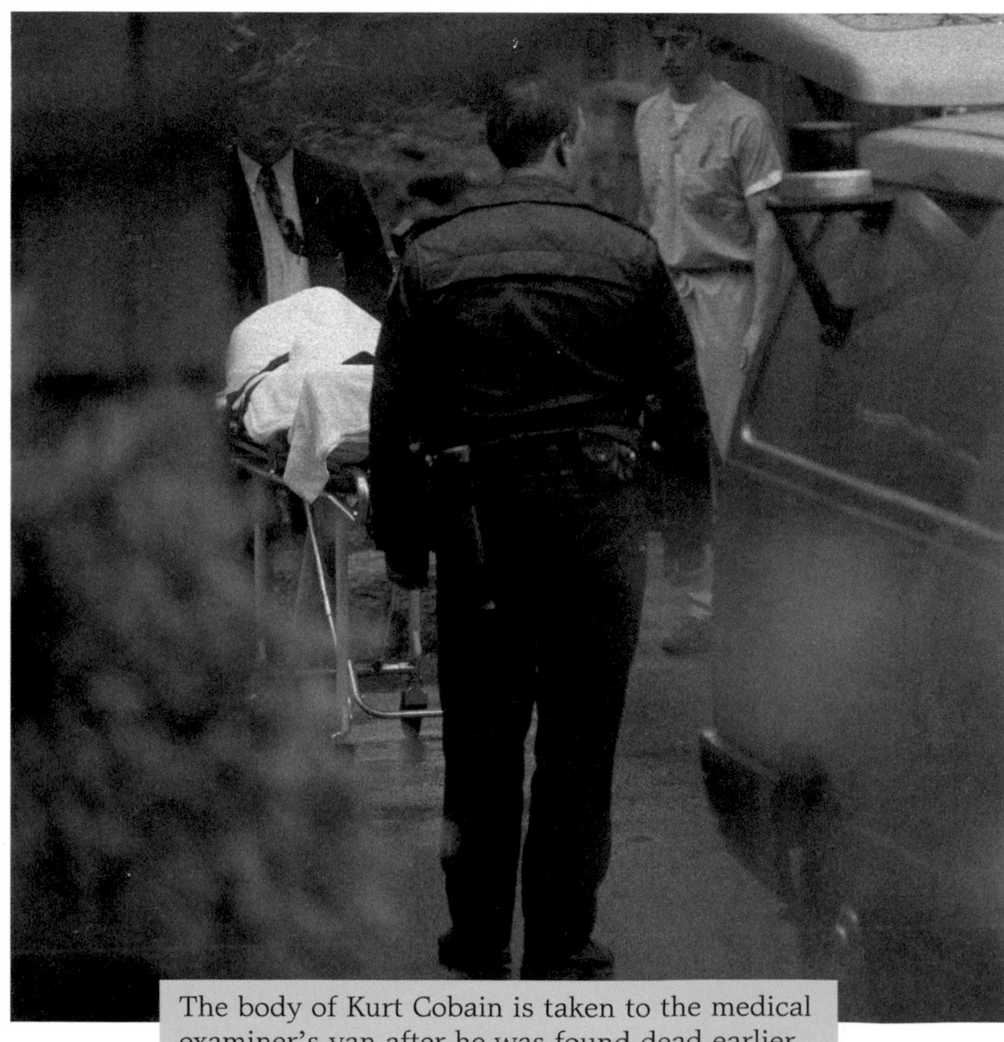

The body of Kurt Cobain is taken to the medical examiner's van after he was found dead earlier that day in his Seattle home.

During that meeting, Cobain's mom gave Barker perhaps the most repeated Cobain-related quote ever. She first said, "I'll never hold him again"[11] and "I was so afraid this was going to happen."[12] After that, she said, "Now he's gone and joined that stupid club. I told him not to join that stupid club."[13] Most media outlets only reprinted the part about the "stupid club." Barker felt that made Cobain's mother sound insensitive and he knew she cared deeply about her son. He had witnessed the outpouring of her emotions and had seen her minutes after she learned of his death. It was obvious to him she was heartbroken.

The "stupid club" referred to a group of popular musicians, like Janis Joplin, Jimi Hendrix, and Jim Morrison of The Doors, who had also died at young ages and were known to abuse drugs. Ironically, all three of those stars had also died at age twenty-seven. Cobain's mom said she blamed his death on the pressures of the music industry and drugs.[14] Her "stupid club" quote was used in a headline on the cover of the July issue of *Esquire* magazine and highlighted in the story itself. The story said Aberdeen is where, "the weight of America bears down with grim, uncushioned brutality."[15] It continued putting the city down, reading, "In many ways, Aberdeen seems like the Land That Time Forgot."[16] The story's tone was so negative that Aberdeen's mayor sent a letter to the magazine. He wrote, "You should be embarrassed at the condescending tone of an article in which you pass judgment on the Cobain family and the residents of Aberdeen in a style reminiscent of a third-rate Tennessee Williams play."[17]

It did not take long for word of Cobain's death to travel the more than one thousand miles to where Love was in Los Angeles. One of Love's friends told her about her husband's death. Love immediately left Los Angeles and she, Frances Bean, and a couple of others flew back to Seattle and went to the house.[18] Fans and media from all over had been hanging outside for hours by the time Love arrived.

LaMont Shillinger, who years before had let Cobain live with him and his family, was recovering from knee surgery in the same hospital where Cobain was born when his doctor woke him to tell him the bad news. Shillinger remembered, "It was some time before I understood that Kurt was dead. I was surprised. I remember being angry that he had taken his own life when he had a child to raise. [My wife] and I were both saddened by his death."[19]

Cobain had talked about dying young before. He and Aberdeen friend Ryan Aigner had even talked about it in casual conversation. Aigner remembers it was in the late 1980s when the two were talking about growing old and what they would be like at age thirty. Cobain said he did not want to be thirty. He said, "I'll never make it to thirty."[20] Aigner later explained what he thought his friend meant by that. He said:

> There was nothing attractive about being thirty. He thought people that were older were dumb.

> He didn't respect their politics, he didn't respect their choices, he didn't like the way they treated each other, didn't like what they did to the planet. Didn't like their prejudices, didn't like their economy. Why join that club?[21]

Earlier on the day Cobain's body was found, a story was published in the *Seattle Post-Intelligencer* about how Nirvana would not be part of the popular summer music festival Lollapalooza, mostly because of concerns over Cobain's health.[22] Instead of Nirvana, the Smashing Pumpkins ended up headlining the show, which also featured the Beastie Boys and Green Day. The best estimate was that Cobain had died a few days before his body was found. The medical examiner listed April 5, 1994 as the date on the death certificate. Determining exactly when someone died is an inexact science, but most people consider April 5 to be the anniversary of his death.

Fans Mourn

With family and friends coming in and out of the house, Love taped a message to Cobain fans. On April 10, it was played at a public memorial vigil at the Seattle Center, near the city's famous Space Needle. About six thousand people showed up with signs and candles. Many wore Nirvana T-shirts and dressed in the grunge wear Cobain helped popularize. During the memorial, some set fire to their flannel shirts, as if saying the days of grunge were over. The event was organized by KXRX, along with rival stations KNDD, and KISW. The stations had always played similar formats and competed hard for Seattle listeners, but put their competition aside and came together to help set up the tribute. A recorded message from Novoselic was played first. Then came Love's, where she read part of Cobain's suicide note, interspersed with her own comments and tears. She said she wished she had been there for her husband.

The effects of Cobain's death were enormous. One twenty-eight-year-old fan in the crowd went home afterward and killed himself with a shotgun.[23] This type of suicide where someone mimics a previous suicide is called a copycat suicide. Shortly after, in the country of Turkey, a sixteen-year-old girl locked herself in a room, played Nirvana music loudly and shot herself in the head.[24] Three years later, two girls in France, ages twelve and thirteen, locked themselves in a room and shot themselves. Their suicide notes mentioned Cobain's death. One friend revealed that the girls said that they "wanted to join Kurt Cobain, but we didn't believe them."[25] Most fans grieved for a long time when Cobain died and several more suicides were linked to Cobain's.

Across town from the public memorial, a private service was held for family and friends. After that service, Love went to the Seattle Center to be with fans there.

Cobain's suicide note later became widely available to the public on the Internet. In it, he said he lost his passion for being in the music industry. He wrote, "I haven't felt the excitement of listening to as well as creating music along with reading and writing for too many years now. I feel guilty beyond words about these things."[26] He also said, "The worst crime I can think of would be to rip people off by faking it and pretending as if I'm having 100% fun. I've tried everything within my power to appreciate it and I do . . . but it's not enough."[27]

He ended the note with a lyric from singer/songwriter Neil Young, "It's better to burn out than to fade away."[28] Young had been trying to reach Cobain in the days before his death, and Cobain had long cited Young as one of his many influences. Many of the songs on Young's *Sleeps With Angels*, the album he was recording when Cobain died, are said to be about Cobain. For years, Young would not speak about the suicide but finally did in 2002. He said, "I was just trying to reach him . . . It's just too bad I didn't get a shot. . . . Only when he used my song in that suicide note was the connection made. Then, I felt it was really unfortunate that I didn't get through to him.[29]

Cobain signed his note, "Peace, love, Empathy. Kurt Cobain."[30]

A memorial vigil had been held in Aberdeen a day before the one in Seattle. There, three hundred people gathered at Morrison Riverfront Park to honor Cobain, many dressed in flannel and holding candles. Local radio station KDUX broadcast the event live and former Nirvana drummer Aaron Burckhard spoke to the crowd. He warned, "Don't try suicide, man. . . . We may play alternative music but suicide is not an alternative."[31]

Almost immediately after Cobain's death, the media came pouring into Seattle, Olympia, and Aberdeen from across the world. All the major TV networks came as did nearly every local and regional media outlet and countless others from out of the country. Everyone was looking for answers, stories, and clues to why Cobain would do this to himself. In just a few short years, his band had gone from playing a beer party in Raymond to international stardom. He had a wife and a young daughter he loved. He had the life most can only dream of, yet he killed himself. People wanted answers.

With the news of Cobain's death, sales of Nirvana merchandise soared and the band's albums rose back up the charts. MTV aired the *Unplugged* show again and again. The funeral-like set suddenly had more meaning. So did his sad blue eyes.

Four days after Cobain's body was found, Hole's album was released. Ironically, the angry album was titled *Live Through This*. One by one, the media left the state, and mourning fans continued on with their lives. They had found their own answers, or had simply given up trying.

A large group of people did not believe Cobain killed himself, giving different explanations as to why they felt that way. Some think Love had him murdered because he was about to ask for a divorce. Many Internet Web sites are devoted entirely to the murder theory. At least two books—*Who Killed Kurt Cobain?* and *Love and Death: The Murder of Kurt Cobain*—have been written about it. In the movie, *Kurt and Courtney*, Love's own father, Hank Harrison, who has also written a book on Cobain, says he thinks Cobain was murdered. Some people discredit his statements because he had been estranged from his daughter since she was little and he never met Cobain.

Tom Grant was the private investigator hired by Love to try and find Cobain when he left the drug rehab center. Grant later said Love's stories did not always add up and were inconsistent. Grant now believes Cobain was murdered. The investigator runs a Web site listing reasons and evidence he says proves the murder took place. On the site, there are also interesting audio snippets of conversations he had with Love around the time of Cobain's death. Many of Grant's suspicions revolve around Love's actions and statements. He said, "When studied carefully, the medical evidence alone proves beyond a reasonable doubt that Kurt Cobain was murdered."[32] One of his main arguments is that Cobain had far more than the lethal amount of heroin is his blood when he died. He argues Cobain would have died almost instantly after injecting that much of the drug and certainly would not have had enough time to shoot himself before being incapacitated. To this day, Grant is investigating the case on his own.

Grant now believes Cobain was murdered.

Some believe the note found by Cobain's body was not really a suicide note but rather a letter to fans saying he was quitting the music business. In Seattle, five days after Cobain's body was found, the host of a public access TV show began talking about how Cobain was murdered. Today, Cobain's death is not the only subject of the show but is still a frequent one. The death was even the focus of an episode of the TV show *Unsolved Mysteries*. Still, there was a history of suicide and tragedy in Cobain's family. Two of his great-uncles had killed themselves. His great-grandfather was a sheriff's deputy who died when his gun accidentally fired. Some members of the family called these tragic deaths the "Cobain Curse." Cobain had even reportedly tried to kill himself once before in Rome. All information considered, suicide is generally the accepted cause of death.

No matter what was true, one fact was clear. Kurt Cobain was dead, and Nirvana would never play another show. What people could not predict is what legacy he and the band would leave behind. Would people soon forget their impact? Or could Cobain and Nirvana stand the test of time?

Chapter 9

An Idol to Many

Nirvana did not fade away after Cobain's death. People were still interested in everything about him and the band. Some even more so than before. In September 1994, Nirvana won another MTV Video Music Award, with "Heart-Shaped Box" awarded Best Alternative Video. The video was very artistic and symbolic, especially so after Cobain's death. It starts out with Cobain, Novoselic, and Grohl sitting in a hospital room while a skinny man, looking like an older version of Cobain, lay sick in a bed across the room. The video shifts through several scenes in a poppy field before ending back in the hospital room. At one point, a young blonde girl opens up a shiny, heart-shaped box and finds it empty.

That November, *Unplugged in New York*, an acoustic album recorded in late 1993 at the MTV *Unplugged* performance, was released. It immediately shot to No. 1 on the *Billboard* charts and also won a Grammy Award for Best Alternative Music Performance.[1] Shortly after, a documentary video called, *Live! Tonight! Sold Out!!* was released. It featured footage from the *Nevermind* tour, including the Dallas incident with Cobain and the bloodied bouncer, and more. Cobain had been very involved with its creation and it has sold more than one million copies.

In 1996, a live Nirvana album was released, called *From the Muddy Banks of the Wishkah*. The Wishkah is the river running through Aberdeen where Cobain was rumored to have spent the night as a teen. Those muddy banks may have inspired Cobain to write "Something in the Way," but the song was not included on the CD. Fans did not seem to care. That album still sold more than a million copies and went to No. 1 on the charts.[2]

When the remaining Nirvana band members began putting together some rare songs for a box set of CDs, trouble arose. Novoselic and Grohl hoped to release it in 2001, the tenth anniversary of *Nevermind*, but Love, who took charge of Cobain's estate after he died, sued the two to stop them from doing it. Most of the disagreement was over a never-before-heard song called "You Know You're Right," which was not quite finished when Cobain died. Nirvana fans worldwide had long discussed the song and wondered what it sounded like. They knew it existed and wanted to hear it. Novoselic and Grohl wanted to release the song on the box set, and Love did not. The two parties fought back and forth through lawyers and the media.

In 2002, a compromise was reached. A greatest hits CD called *Nirvana* was released with "You Know You're Right" as its first song. In the chorus, Cobain screams the word "pain" for almost ten seconds. The single disc included many of the hit songs Nirvana had released, though many others were left off. A four-disc box set, called *With The Lights Out*, which was a lyric from "Smells Like Teen Spirit," followed in 2004. It featured three CDs of rare Nirvana recordings, many never heard before, and one DVD of old footage. The first CD began with a poorly recorded song from Nirvana's first show

Though his musical career only lasted a short while, Kurt Cobain is still fondly remembered for his music, which continues to reach every new generation.

at the house party in Raymond and the last CD ended with Cobain alone on acoustic guitar singing "All Apologies." In between were fifty-nine other tracks, many never before heard and several "rough drafts" with just Cobain, a guitar, and a poor audio recorder capturing the moment. Even the unfinished version of "Pen Cap Chew" from the 1988 session with Jack Endino, where the tape had run out before the song was finished, was included. Endino said, "It actually ran out just as the second chorus was starting, but the only way to save it was to fade it and make it half a song."[3] Other highlights from the collection include "Old Age" and "Do Re Mi," a roughly recorded song featuring just Cobain and a guitar at his home. The song's soft sound is reminiscent of the *Unplugged* concert, recorded just a few months prior to "Do Re Mi."

One of the DVD's main features was a never-before-seen practice session from 1988, held in an apartment above Novoselic's mom's hair salon in Aberdeen. A cousin sued Novoselic over the footage, claiming she loaned it to Novoselic and he promised to pay her for it but never had. *With the Lights Out* sold more than one million copies in less than three months even though the average price was around fifty dollars. In 2005, a single CD culled from the box set, *Sliver: The Best of the Box*, was released with "Spank Thru" from the revered *Fecal Matter* recording as its first track. Some fans were not happy with either release. They believed Cobain would not have wanted his unfinished songs heard.

Many of those same fans had been equally outraged three years earlier, when several notebooks filled with Cobain's incomplete song lyrics, drawings, unsent letters, and more were released in book form. The book was simply called *Journals*. The upset fans brandished the same argument, that Cobain would not have wanted his unfinished works to be viewed by anyone. A note written years earlier by Cobain himself seemed to address the topic in the first page of *Journals*. He wrote, "Don't read my diary when I'm gone."[4] But further down the page he wrote, "when you wake up this morning, please read my diary. Look through my things, and figure me out."[5] Figuring Cobain out was difficult; he often did not even know what he wanted.

An artsy movie loosely based on Cobain's life, *Last Days*, was released in 2005. The next year, filming began on a Cobain documentary that was to use the rock star's own voice—taken from audio interviews recorded by the author of a Nirvana biography—as its only narration. Dozens of documentaries have been made over the years, most of average quality.

The Best of All-time?

Nevermind, the album that brought Nirvana and dozens of similar-sounding bands into the mainstream, has now sold more than 14 million copies. It and Nirvana have won countless "best of all-time" awards handed out by newspapers, magazines, and television networks. *Nevermind* has been voted best album of all time by MTV and "Smells Like Teen Spirit" was named the network's greatest music video ever. Cobain was named *Rolling Stone*'s "Artist of the Decade" for the 1990s. In 2003, "Smells Like Teen Spirit" was VH1's top song of the past twenty-five years. Worldwide, Nirvana has sold more than 50 million albums, and the honors keep coming.[6]

On a smaller scale, controversies surrounding Cobain's death began almost immediately in his hometown. First, the organizers of Lollapalooza considered staging a show in Hoquiam in honor of Cobain. The city council hosted a public hearing to discuss the matter. Councilman Jim Eddy phoned Novoselic, who said he would come and speak. Nearly seven hundred people showed up, most in favor of the event coming to town. Some people were hesitant because Cobain had said many bad things about the area in the media. A lot of locals did not like him for that reason. Novoselic tried to clear that up, saying, "There is this perception that Kurt Cobain hated Aberdeen. That made a really good media story, but it wasn't true. . . . We've been all around the world and there's a little bit of Aberdeen everywhere."[7] Novoselic continued talking in support of the event coming to town. The city's police chief did not feel it would be safe to hold the event. He thought the estimated twenty-five thousand people would be too overwhelming and cause too much damage to homes close to the stadium. He was concerned over public safety issues and crowd control. While the council debated, and eventually approved the concert, the promoters decided to stage the event elsewhere.

Another controversy started when a local artist created a statue of Cobain. She wanted to put it on public display. Some people spoke out against it because they did not want kids to idolize someone who used drugs and committed suicide. They felt Cobain was not someone to be proud of. Novoselic did not like the idea of the statue, either. He sent a letter to the newspaper saying it would only serve as a "shrine for idolaters to prostrate themselves in front of and a beacon for reactionaries to shake their fists at while cursing."[8] He continued, "I'll knock that statue down. I have no other choice. To let it stand would signal the defeat of all that we tried to make happen."[9] Today, the statue remains with the artist.

The Band Played On

Nirvana's surviving members have gone in different directions. Novoselic has done a little bit of everything. He said, "I feel like people's connection with Nirvana has propelled me into a role of many definitions."[10] He has started a few other bands, including Sweet 75 and Eyes Adrift, which included one member of the Meat Puppets and one from a popular 1990s ska band, Sublime, whose singer died of a heroin overdose. In 1995, Novoselic founded JAMPAC, or Joint Artists and Music Promotions Political Action Committee. It was a nonprofit group that spoke out for the rights of people involved in the music industry. Novoselic divorced his first wife and has since remarried. He also wrote a book called *Of Grunge and Government: Let's Fix This Broken Democracy* and has remained active in local politics. In 2004, he considered running for lieutenant governor of the State of Washington before eventually deciding against it.

The year after Cobain's death, Grohl put together a band called the Foo Fighters, which has sold millions of albums. The Foo Fighters' first album contained songs Grohl had been working on for his own enjoyment at the time of Cobain's death. On the self-titled album, Grohl played most of the instruments and sang. When the band played live, Grohl played guitar and sang. The rest of the band included former Nirvana touring guitarist Pat Smear and two members of the just-broken-up Sub Pop band, Sunny Day Real Estate. After some lineup changes, the Foo Fighters have released four more albums and are still a hit today. Some of their more popular songs include "Everlong," "Learn to Fly," "Next Year," "Best of You," and "My Hero," a sentimental tune many believe is written about Cobain. Over the years, Grohl has also played with several side-projects, including Queens of the Stone Age. He also put together a collection of superstar heavy metal singers onto one album with an all-star project called Probot. The singers were many of Grohl's all-time favorites.

Courtney Love had both big wins and losses after Cobain's death. She began acting again, winning several awards and earning a nomination for a coveted Golden Globe Award. It was for her role in *The People vs. Larry Flynt*, in which she played the wife of Flynt, a controversial adult magazine publisher. She also continued battling drug addiction and for custody of

Frances Bean. Love was in trouble several times for various crimes, including felony drug charges, for allegedly hitting a man in the head with a microphone and for attempting to break into her boyfriend's house. Her band Hole had two Platinum albums before breaking up in 2001. Love released a solo album in 2004, called *America's Sweetheart* that did not sell as well as her other records.

In 2006, Love sold 25 percent of her share of Nirvana's music catalog for more than 50 million dollars. Some fear that move will increase the use of Nirvana's songs in movies, television commercials, and more, which many fans think Cobain would not have wanted. She also announced plans to release her own book, *Love Diaries: My Life in Words and Pictures*. The book will be similar to Cobain's *Journals*, and will include unpublished writings, love letters to her husband, and rare photos of the couple and young Frances Bean.

Frances herself is now being seen more in public. She has been featured in magazine interviews and photo shoots and spotted in the crowd of popular television shows like American Idol. Now a teenager, the girl's resemblance to her father is instantly recognizable.

In 2004, the tenth anniversary of Cobain's death, three Aberdeen High School students wrote a story for *The (Aberdeen) Daily World*'s teen section. They wondered why the city had not done anything to honor Cobain and wrote, "It's now been nearly a decade since Cobain's death. It's time for a local tribute to Kurt Cobain."[11]

Two adults read the story and decided to form a group to discuss the matter. Naming themselves the Kurt Cobain Memorial Committee, the eight-member group, which included Kurt Cobain's grandfather, Leland Cobain, held community meetings, brainstorming ways to honor Cobain in Aberdeen. The group first decided to replace the city's welcome sign, adding the words "Come As You Are" in 2005. The words were chosen because they were the name of the popular Nirvana song and because even people who did not know about Nirvana could relate to them. The nonprofit organization's future plans include a memorial park and a youth center for teens, both in Cobain's name.

Each year, Aberdeen High School gives out a varying number of Kurt Cobain Visual Arts Scholarships to graduating seniors who are not necessarily the straight-A students. The college scholarships were created soon after Cobain died by his mom, wife, and the band. Cobain's former art teacher Bob Hunter and Cobain's former boarder, LaMont Shillinger, are the administrators. Hunter believes it is the largest high school art endowment in Washington State.

What once was a single, half-empty file folder in the Aberdeen library is now an alphabetized, multi-folder series, featuring hundreds of articles on Nirvana. They sit in a back corner of the library's second floor, locked away in the drawer of a file cabinet. It is almost as difficult to view the files as it is to gain access to a guarded government building. That is because they have been stolen numerous times by fans looking for souvenirs.

Twelve years after his death, Kurt Cobain's influences are found not only in his home state, but also worldwide. When a band writes a song with quiet verses followed by powerfully loud choruses, there is a good chance they have been influenced by Nirvana. Kids who wear flannel shirts and ripped jeans to school are unknowingly influenced by Cobain's way of dress. In death, Cobain has become similar to one of his heroes, John Lennon of the Beatles. Like Cobain, Lennon was a popular musician who died in the prime of his life. Lennon was shot and killed at age forty by an obsessed fan.

Many musicians have rerecorded Nirvana's music. Rocks bands like Evanescence, Papa Roach, Limp Bizkit, and Velvet Revolver have performed their songs. Even 1950s teen idol Paul Anka released a version of "Smells Like Teen Spirit" on his 2005 album. It sounded nothing like Nirvana's version, but helped put the aging artist back in the spotlight. Over the years, several amateur cover bands have sprung up that only play Nirvana songs.

More unreleased Nirvana songs are rumored to still exist. When and if they are released, the public will surely buy them. There are dozens of fan Web sites dedicated to Cobain and Nirvana. Though the band has not been together since the mid-1990s, the sites are still active, updated with related news as it happens, and filled with message board posts from people from across the world. Many want to know more about how a sheltered kid from a small town changed the music world forever. Novoselic said:

> The deification of Kurt Cobain is a phenomenon in itself. This phenomenon has played itself through human history with many personalities. The lesson for me is to let people have their idols and to stay out of the way. The popularity of Nirvana and the effect the band has had . . . is profound.[12]

Each April 5, people travel from around the world to pay respects to Cobain. In Seattle, they go to Viretta Park, located next to the house he died in. In Aberdeen, they get their picture taken at the "Come As You Are" sign at the city limits and tour the homes of his youth, his schools, and to the bridge Cobain said he once slept under on the muddy banks of the Wishkah River. The underside of the bridge is covered with graffiti from fans. There are half-burned candles, flowers, and cards—all thanking Cobain for giving them music that helped them conquer one personal problem or another.

Grohl said:

> I listen to the music now and think we were a pretty cool band. But do I think that it's worth the "legendary" status that people seem to believe in? No. It's just a band . . . It's always the ones who die young that people remember for some reason. . . . You're left with just some sort of question mark—and it lasts forever.[13] Kurt's become a legend, but he was just a man.[14]

To his former bandmate this may be true, but Kurt Cobain will always be an idol to many.

Author's Note

Kurt Cobain is proof—greatness can be found anywhere.

It could be the boy in the next seat in high school that everyone makes fun of or the poor girl stuck at a rainy bus stop because her parents cannot afford a car. It could even be the person in the mirror.

For me, greatness was still sleeping at noon on a couch in Aberdeen, Washington in the fall of 1985. That is where I first saw Kurt Cobain. I didn't think much of him. I was on lunch break from high school, hanging out with my friend, Eric Shillinger. Kurt was a high school dropout living on Eric's couch. On subsequent lunches, the three of us walked around town and visited thrift stores and pawn shops together. After school, I would sometimes see Kurt at practices for the Melvins. By that time, Kurt was becoming a Melvins' insider. I was barely cool enough to stick my nose in the door.

In hindsight, I wish I remembered more. What did Kurt say? What did he admire in the thrift store? Was he looking for an obscure punk rock album or another ripped pair of blue jeans? Unfortunately, Kurt did not affect me much then. He was just another guy, and guys tend to forget things about other guys.

The next year, I learned Kurt was in a band. One day in class, his sister, Kim, offered me a recording of his music but I didn't take it. I assumed it would be bad and it *definitely* could not have been as cool as what I was listening to. Which was funny because I was listening to bands like the Melvins and early songs from Soundgarden and Green River, mixed with the heavy metal of Slayer, Motörhead, and Aberdeen's own Metal Church. Toss in a few pop-rock guilty pleasures, and it is apparent to me now. A mixture of all my favorite elements of those bands was what Kurt's band was. But I couldn't be bothered with getting to know it at the time.

Still, I felt a sense of pride when *Nevermind* hit it big and I saw Kurt on MTV. I was away at college but my real friends knew I was from Aberdeen. They quickly associated me with Nirvana and asked me for stories. Most of the time, I told them what little I had.

Then Kurt died.

As I would later with the Oklahoma City bombing, the death of relatives, and 9-11, I remember exactly where I was when I heard the news. I didn't want to tell my "rock star" story anymore. Sure, I might have had the posters on the wall, the CDs in the rack, the dyed hair and flannel shirts but that didn't mean I wanted to talk about it.

Time eventually healed most of the sadness. I moved back to Aberdeen, as Kurt once said he might so he could again fade into obscurity. In 2003, my brother, Andy, won a Kurt Cobain Visual Arts Scholarship from Aberdeen High School. The next year, I helped establish the Kurt Cobain Memorial Committee. With my longtime friend and now city councilman, Paul Fritts, as a partner, I forged through public meetings, tons of paperwork, and the occasional anonymous threat. Finally, I, Paul, and the other committee members were able to recognize Kurt publicly in Aberdeen.

There's now a neat new sign at the entrance of town welcoming visitors to "Come As You Are." We've got more projects in the works, including a park and a youth center. Finding the fine line between what we think Kurt would be okay with (always a tricky task)

and what he wouldn't is not easy. We're constantly in touch with diehard fans across the globe and often take their advice.

We also battle some bitterness toward Kurt from residents who believe he hated Aberdeen, based on what he said to the media. I believe he was just doing as myself and most of my friends had done. Teens everywhere grow tired of their hometowns and long to cxplorc. Thcy think the grass is always greener but most opinions never make it beyond a group of friends. Kurt's were written down and spread to millions.

In spite of it all, we know we must be doing fine so far. Many people, even Kurt's mother, have thanked us for our efforts. His grandfather, Leland Cobain, is one of our most enthusiastic committee members. People log onto our Web site (see "Internet Addresses" section on page 154) from across the world.

It's been a humbling process. My story is just one of thousands of similar tales—stories of how a life was greatly impacted by the passionate art created by a skinny, introverted kid from a small town in the middle of nowhere who went on to change the course of music history.

—Jeff Burlingame

Chronology

1967—Kurt Donald Cobain born on February 20 in Aberdeen, Washington; lives with family in neighboring city of Hoquiam; moves with family to Aberdeen in August.

1970—Sister, Kimberly, born in April.

1976—Parents separate shortly after his ninth birthday, divorce four months later.

1977—Moves in with his father in Montesano.

1981—Begins to make home movies, including one called *Kurt Commits Bloody Suicide*; tries marijuana for the first time; gets electric guitar from uncle and takes lessons; wrestles and competes in track at Montesano High School.

1982—Moves from Montesano to Aberdeen, living with various relatives; transfers to Aberdeen High School and begins taking art classes.

1983—Discovers the Melvins and begins attending the band's practices; discovers love for punk rock music.

1984—Moves in with friend Jesse Reed's family in North River.

1985—Leaves Reed house, gets apartment in Aberdeen and works various jobs; allegedly spends nights under bridge; moves in with Shillinger family.

1986—Arrested by police for vandalism; records "Fecal Matter" demo with Dale Crover; arrested by police for trespassing; leaves Shillinger house;

forms band with bassist Krist Novoselic; moves into first house on his own in Aberdeen with Matt Lukin of the Melvins, practicing music there.

1987—Begins dating Tracy Marander; plays first show with Novoselic and drummer Aaron Burckhard at house party in Raymond, Washington; moves into Marander's apartment in Olympia, Washington; performs with band on college radio station and at many regional concerts.

1988—Records demo in Seattle with producer Jack Endino; fires Burckhard and adds drummer Dave Foster to the band; chooses final band name of Nirvana; music played on college radio station; replaces Foster with drummer Chad Channing; first story written about Nirvana; "Love Buzz"/ "Big Cheese" single released on Sub Pop Records.

1989—Nirvana's first album, *Bleach*, released; tours West Coast then across the United States with second guitarist Jason Everman; fires Everman, then Nirvana goes on first overseas tour; Nirvana performs on DJ John Peel's radio show.

1990—Records demos in Wisconsin with producer Butch Vig; breaks up with Tracy Marander; fires Chad Channing, temporarily replacing him with Dan Peters of Mudhoney then permanently with Dave Grohl; "Sliver"/"Dive" single released on Sub Pop.

1991—First plays "Smells Like Teen Spirit" in concert; Nirvana signs with Geffen Records; "Smells Like Teen Spirit" single and video released in the beginning of September; *Nevermind* released on

September 24, debuting at No. 144 on *Billboard* charts; begins dating Courtney Love; *Nevermind* goes Gold in October; *Nevermind* goes Platinum in November.

1992—*Nevermind* goes double Platinum in January and hits No. 1 on the *Billboard* charts; Nirvana performs on *Saturday Night Live*; *Nevermind* goes triple Platinum in February; "Come As You Are" video released in February; marries Courtney Love on February 24 in Hawaii; *Nevermind* goes quadruple Platinum in June; controversial article published in *Vanity Fair* magazine; checks into a hospital to kick a heroin habit; daughter Frances Bean Cobain born on August 18; wins two awards at MTV Video Music Awards; *Incesticide* released.

1993—*In Utero* debuts at No. 1 on Billboard charts; second *Saturday Night Live* performance; *Come As You Are* biography released; Nirvana performs on *MTV Unplugged* show; Nirvana performs for MTV's *Live and Loud* series.

1994—Wal-Mart and Kmart ban *In Utero* from stores; plays last show in March; overdoses in Rome on March 3; police called to Cobain's Seattle home and confiscate his guns on March 18; attends drug intervention on March 25; enters drug treatment in Los Angeles on March 30, fleeing two days later; becomes subject of missing persons report on April 4; found dead at home by electrician on April 8; *In Utero* goes triple Platinum; Nirvana wins MTV Video Music Award for "Heart-Shaped Box;" *Unplugged in New York* released.

1996—*From the Muddy Banks of the Wishkah* live album released, hitting No. 1 on the *Billboard* charts.

1999—"Rape Me" released on *Saturday Night Live: The Musical Performances, Vol. 2*; Nirvana is named *Rolling Stone*'s artist of the decade for the 1990s.

2002—Greatest hits CD *Nirvana* released with new song, "You Know You're Right."

2004—*With The Lights Out* box set released.

2005—*Sliver: The Best of the Box* released.

Chapter Notes

Chapter 1. Live and Not Loud

1. Alan di Perna, "Season Finale: Behind Unplugged," *Guitar World*, March 1995 <http://www.nirvanafreak.net/art/art18.shtml> (January 6, 2006).
2. Rasmus Holmen, "Alex Coletti Interview," *The Internet Nirvana Fan Club*, 2000, <http://www.nirvanafanclub.com> (May 10, 2005).
3. Personal interview with Leland Cobain, April 4, 2004.
4. David Fricke, "Kurt Cobain: The Rolling Stone Interview," in *Cobain by the Editors of Rolling Stone* (New York: Rolling Stone Press, 1994), p. 64.

Chapter 2. Metamorphosis

1. Charles Cross, *Heavier Than Heaven: A Biography of Kurt Cobain* (New York: Hyperion, 2001), p. 9.
2. Gillian Gaar, "Verse Chorus Verse: The Recording History of Nirvana," *Goldmine*, February 14, 1997, <http://www.nirvanafanclub.com> (January 27, 2005).
3. Michael Azerrad, *Come As You Are: The Story of Nirvana* (New York: Main Street Books, Doubleday, 1993), p. 15
4. Ibid.
5. Personal interview with Leland Cobain, April 4, 2004.
6. Ibid.
7. Ibid.

8. Azerrad, p. 18.
9. Ibid., p. 17.
10. Ibid.
11. Personal interview with Leland Cobain, February 7, 2005.
12. Ibid.
13. Cross, p. 32.
14. Ibid, p. 33.
15. Personal interview with Warren Mason, April 10, 2005.
16. Ibid.
17. Ibid.
18. Azerrad, p. 23.
19. Phil West, title unknown, *The Daily*, University of Washington, May 5, 1989, <http://www.nirvanafanclub.com> (March 26, 2005).
20. Personal interview with Leland Cobain, April 10, 2005.
21. Ibid.
22. Ibid.
23. Kurt Cobain, *Journals* (New York: Riverhead Books, 2002), p. 27.
24. Azerrad, p. 33.
25. Personal interview with Bob Hunter, May 19, 2005.
26. Ibid.
27. Ibid.
28. Ibid.
29. Ibid.
30. E-mail interview with Buzz Osborne, May 4, 2000.
31. Ibid.
32. Personal interview with Dave Reed, June 2003.

33. Ibid.
34. Ibid.
35. Personal interview with LaMont Shillinger, June 1, 2005.
36. Ibid.
37. Ibid.
38. Personal interview with Ryan Aigner, June 4, 2005.
39. Ibid.

Chapter 3. Finding "Nirvana"

1. Personal interview with Ryan Aigner, June 4, 2005.
2. Ibid.
3. "Kurt Speaks, An Exclusive 1994 interview," *VH1.com*, n.d., <http://www.vh1.com/artists/interview/1458484/11042002/nirvana.jhtml> (June 20, 2005).
4. Personal interview with Ryan Aigner, June 4, 2005.
5. Ibid.
6. Michael Azerrad, *Come As You Are: The Story of Nirvana* (New York: Main Street Books, Doubleday, 1993), p. 62.
7. Ibid, p. 66.
8. Ibid, p. 236.
9. Personal interview with Jack Endino, December 18, 2005.
10. Personal interview with Jack Endino, June 11, 2005.
11. Personal interview with Jack Endino, December 18, 2005.
12. Carrie Borzillo, *Nirvana: The Day-By-Day Eyewitness Chronicle* (New York: Thunder's Mouth Press, 2000), p. 20.

13. Personal interview with Jack Endino, June 11, 2005.
14. *Webster's New World Dictionary*, 3rd college ed. (New York: Simon and Schuster, 1988), p. 918.
15. Charles Cross, *Heavier Than Heaven: A Biography of Kurt Cobain* (New York: Hyperion, 2001), p. 100.
16. Dawn Anderson, "It May Be The Devil," *Backlash*, September 1988, <http://www.nirvanafanclub.com> (April 18, 2005).
17. Kurt Cobain, *Journals*, (New York: Riverhead Books, 2002), p. 16.
18. *Kurt Cobain: The Early Life of a legend*, DVD, Chrome Dreams Media, 2004.
19. Personal interview with Jack Endino, June 11, 2005.
20. Azerrad, p. 87

Chapter 4. Grunge Rock

1. Everett True, "Ten Myths About Seattle Exploded," in *Uncut Legends #2: Kurt Cobain* (London: IPC Media, 2004), p. 48.
2. Allison M. Rosen, "Don't Say the G-Word: Or Mudhoney will punch you in the face)," August 23–29, 2002, <http://www.ocf.berkeley.edu/~ptn/mudhoney/articles/20020823oc.html> (February 1, 2006).
3. Personal interview with Robb Bates, May 13, 2005.
4. Ibid.
5. Personal interview with Jack Endino, June 11, 2005.

6. Personal interview with Jack Endino, December 18, 2005.
7. Everett True, "Tad and Nirvana: The Larder They Come," *Melody Maker*, March 17, 1990, <http://www.nirvanafanclub.com> (April 24, 2005).
8. *Kurt Cobain: The Early Life of a Legend*, DVD, Chrome Dreams Media, 2004.
9. Radio interview with Kurt Cobain, March 27, 1990 on WOZQ FM, <http://www.nirvanafanclub.com> (March 14, 2005).
10. *Kurt Cobain: The Early Life of a Legend*, DVD, Chrome Dreams Media, 2004
11. Carrie Borzillo, *Nirvana: The Day-By-Day Eyewitness Chronicle* (New York: Thunder's Mouth Press, 2000), p. 40.
12. Michael Azerrad, *Come As You Are: The Story of Nirvana* (New York: Main Street Books, Doubleday, 1993), p. 108.
13. Borzillo, p. 48.
14. E-mail interview with Greg Kot, May 14, 2005.
15. *Nirvana Live Guide—1990*, <http://www.nirvanaguide.com/1990.php> (April 24, 2005).
16. Charles Cross, *Heavier Than Heaven: A Biography of Kurt Cobain* (New York: Hyperion, 2001), p. 153.

Chapter 5. Smells Like Success

1. Brad Morrell, *Nirvana & the Sound of Seattle* (London: Omnibus Press, 1993), p. 80.
2. Ibid., p. 81.
3. *Nirvana: Nevermind Classic Albums*, DVD, Isis Productions/Eagle Rock Entertainment, 2004.

4. Keith Cameron, title unavailable, *Sounds*, October, 1990, <http://www.nirvanafanclub.com> (April 28, 2005).
5. Michael Azerrad, *Come As You Are: The Story of Nirvana* (New York: Main Street Books, Doubleday, 1993), p. 156.
6. *Nirvana: Nevermind Classic Albums*, DVD, Isis Productions/Eagle Rock Entertainment, 2004.
7. Charles Cross, *Heavier Than Heaven: A Biography of Kurt Cobain* (New York: Hyperion, 2001), p. 171.
8. Azerrad, p. 165.
9. Ibid.
10. Ibid.
11. Carrie Borzillo, *Nirvana: The Day-By-Day Eyewitness Chronicle* (New York: Thunder's Mouth Press, 2000), p. 68.
12. Azerrad, p. 168.
13. Jim Berkenstadt and Charles Cross, "*Nevermind: Nirvana*," (New York: Schirmer Books, 1998) p. 109.
14. Borzillo, p. 76.
15. Wendy O'Connor, "Local 'twanger' makes good, mom reports," *The (Aberdeen) Daily World*, November 21, 1991, p. A4.
16. Ibid.
17. Ibid.

Chapter 6. Dethroning the King

1. Charles Cross, *Heavier Than Heaven: A Biography of Kurt Cobain* (New York: Hyperion, 2001), p. 220.
2. Claude Iosso, "Local boys reach Nirvana," *The (Aberdeen) Daily World*, January 21, 1992, p. A1.

3. Ibid.
4. Personal interview with Ryan Aigner, June 4, 2005.
5. Poppy Z. Brite, *Courtney Love* (New York: Simon & Schuster, 1997), p. 132.
6. Michael Azerrad, *Come As You Are: The Story of Nirvana* (New York: Main Street Books, Doubleday, 1993), p. 252.
7. Dave McLean "Dave Grohl: Grohl With It," <http://enjoyment.independent.co.uk/music/features/article224944.ece> (February 1, 2006).
8. Personal interview with Leland Cobain, February 7, 2005.
9. *Kurt Cobain: The Early Life of a legend*, DVD, Chrome Dreams Media, 2004.

Chapter 7. Bored and Old

1. Kevin Allman, "Nirvana's Front Man Shoots from the Hip," *The Advocate*, February 9, 1993, <http://www.nirvanafreak.net/art/art5.shtml> (April 30, 2005).
2. Personal interview with Leland Cobain, February 7, 2005.
3. David Fricke, "Kurt Cobain: The Rolling Stone Interview," in *Cobain by the Editors of Rolling Stone* (New York: Rolling Stone Press, 1994), p. 68.
4. Laurence Romance, "I Want to Go Solo—Like Johnny Cash," in *Uncut Legends #2: Kurt Cobain* (London: IPC Media, 2004), p. 100.
5. *The Smoking Gun*, <http://www.thesmokinggun.com/archive/kurtdrug2.html> (June 3, 2005).
6. Ibid.
7. *The Smoking Gun*, <http://www.thesmokinggun.com/archive/kurtfight2.htm> (June 3, 2005).

8. John Mulvey, "Nevermind the Sell-Out," in *Uncut Legends #2: Kurt Cobain* (London: IPC Media, 2004), p. 63.
9. Romance, p. 104.
10. E-mail interview with Cyndy (Counts) Hayes, April 21, 2005.
11. Ibid.
12. Ibid.
13. Jolie Lash, "The Producers: Alex Coletti," *Uncut Legends #2: Kurt Cobain* (London: IPC Media, 2004), p. 122.
14. Chuck Crisafulli, *Teen Spirit: The Stories Behind Every Nirvana Song* (New York: Fireside, 1996), p. 123.
15. Kathryn Crawford, "I don't have the passion any more," originally published in *The New York Times*, repr. April 11, 1994 *The (Aberdeen) Daily World*, p. A7.
16. Charles Cross, *Heavier Than Heaven: A Biography of Kurt Cobain* (New York: Hyperion, 2001), p. 311.
17. Claude Iosso, "Doctors optimistic singer will fully recover," *The (Aberdeen) Daily World*, March 5, 1994, p. A7.
18. Ibid.
19. *The Smoking Gun*, <http://www.thesmokinggun.com/archive/kurtmarchrep2.html> (June 4, 2005).
20. Ibid.
21. Cross, pp. 330–331.
22. Poppy Z. Brite, *Courtney Love* (New York: Simon & Schuster, 1997), p. 171
23. *The Smoking Gun*, <http://www.thesmokinggun.com/archive/kurtmissing1.html> (June 6, 2005).

Chapter 8. Joining a "Stupid Club"

1. Steven Goldsmith, Dan Rayley, and Jane Hadley, "Cobain's Suicide Note Ended With 'I Love You'—Gunshot Death Shocks Nirvana Fans, But Some Say They Saw It Coming," *Seattle Post-Intelligencer*, April 9, 1994, p. A1.
2. Tom Grant, "The Kurt Cobain Murder Investigation," <http://www.cobaincase.com/events.htm#2>, (August 10, 2005).
3. E-mail interview with Marty Riemer, May 26, 2005.
4. Ibid.
5. Ibid.
6. Ibid.
7. Ibid.
8. Personal interview with Doug Barker, June 2, 2005.
9. Ibid.
10. Ibid.
11. Doug Barker and Claude Iosso, "Nirvana's Cobain dead at 28 [sic]," *The (Aberdeen) Daily World*, April 8, 1994, p. A1.
12. Ibid.
13. Ibid.
14. Ibid.
15. Stephen Wright, "The Big No," *Esquire*, July 1994, p. 56.
16. Ibid.
17. Chuck Gurrad, Aberdeen, Washington, Letter to *Esquire* editor from Aberdeen mayor, July 7, 1994.
18. Poppy Z. Brite, *Courtney Love* (New York: Simon & Schuster, 1997), pp. 175–176.

19. Personal interview with LaMont Shillinger, June 1, 2005.
20. Personal interview with Ryan Aigner, June 4, 2005.
21. Ibid.
22. Gene Stout, "Lollapalooza '94 To Tour Without Nirvana," *Seattle Post-Intelligencer*, April 8, 1994, p. 10.
23. Steve Dougherty, "No Way Out," *People*, April 25, 1994, p. 44.
24. Anthony DeCurtis, "A Cry in the Dark" *Rolling Stone*, June 2, 1994, p. 40.
25. "French girls kill themselves to 'join' Cobain," *The (Aberdeen Daily World)*, May 16, 1997, p. B7.
26. *Justice for Kurt*, <http://www.justiceforkurt.com/investigation/documents/note_scan.shtml>, (June 11, 2005).
27. Ibid.
28. DeCurtis, p. 43
29. Burhan Wazir, "Neil Young, the Quiet Achiever," *The Guardian*, May 11, 2002, <http://www.smh.com.au/articles/2002/05/10/1021002387905.html>, (June 10, 2005).
30. *Justice For Kurt*, <http://www.justiceforkurt.com/investigation/documents/note_scan.shtml>, (June 11, 2005).
31. Claude Iosso, "300 honor Cobain in candlelight vigil," *The (Aberdeen) Daily World*, April 10, 1994, p. A1.
32. Tom Grant, "The Kurt Cobain Murder Investigation," <http://www.cobaincase.com/events.htm#2> (June 20, 2005).

Chapter 9. An Idol to Many

1. Martin C. Strong, *The Great Rock Discography* (Edinburgh, England: Canongate Books, 2002), p. 753.
2. Ibid.
3. Personal interview with Jack Endino, June 11, 2005.
4. Kurt Cobain, *Journals* (New York: Riverhead Books, 2002), book preface.
5. Ibid.
6. *The Internet Nirvana Fan Club*, <http://www.nirvanafanclub.com> (May 10, 2005).
7. Doug Barker, "It's a media myth that Cobain hated Aberdeen, Nirvana bassist tells crowd," *The (Aberdeen) Daily World*, April 27, 1994, p. A1.
8. Krist Novoselic, "'Kurt would hate the idea of a statue,' says Nirvana bandmate," *The (Aberdeen) Daily World*, July 7, 1994, p. A4.
9. Ibid.
10. Personal interview with Krist Novoselic, May 23, 1999.
11. Clare Powers, Corrie Powers, and Elisha Hagedorn, "Where's Nirvana," *The (Aberdeen) Daily World*, February 29, 2004, p. B5.
12. Personal interview with Krist Novoselic, May 23, 1999.
13. "The 'legendary' Nirvana were really just another band, reckons Dave Grohl," in *Uncut Legends #2: Kurt Cobain* (London: IPC Media, 2004), p. 18.
14. Dave Grohl, *Kerrang!*, <http://www.nirvanaclub.com> (March 11, 2005).

Glossary

alternative music—A type of rock 'n' roll music, rooted in punk rock, that does not fit into the mainstream.

anarchy—A situation, often political, filled with disorder or confusion.

Associated Press (AP)—Based in the United States, it is the world's largest news organization.

Billboard—A magazine devoted to the music industry.

bouncer—A doorman who helps control crowds at performances.

chord—Three or more musical notes played on an instrument at the same time.

compilation—An album consisting of a collection of songs performed by one or more artists.

cover—A new version of a previously recorded song.

demo—A recording made for personal use rather than release to the public.

disc jockey—An individual who plays music for an audience, especially on the radio. Also known as a deejay or DJ.

fanzine—A small magazine intended only for fans of a particular subject.

45—A type of vinyl musical record, usually containing one song on each side. So named because it spins on a player at 45 revolutions per minute.

Generation X—A generic name for the group of Americans born from 1965 through 1975. Members of the group were often perceived as rebellious, self-absorbed, shallow, and not as hard working as their elders.

gold album—A music album that has sold a minimum of five hundred thousand copies.

Grammy—An annual honor given by the Recording Academy for outstanding achievements in the recording industry. Awarded in several categories, it is the musical equivalent of an Academy Award.

grunge—A form of alternative music featuring hard drumming, heavy guitar sounds, and loud vocals. A slowed-down version of punk rock literally meaning "dirty, messy or unpleasant."

hair band—A heavy metal group said to be more, or at least equally, concerned with fashion than music.

heavy metal—A form of music characterized by loud playing, distorted instruments, and screamed vocals.

heroin—A dangerous and addictive drug, illegal in the United States and many other countries. It is derived from the opium poppy plant.

liner notes—Notes inside a record, cassette, or CD explaining what is on the album. Often includes production information, thank-yous, and song lyrics.

nirvana—Any place or condition of great peace and happiness.

overdose—The ingestion of too much of a substance, generally some type of drug.

platinum album—A music album having sold a minimum of one million copies.

pop music—Any genre of music that is commercially friendly and marketable, often featuring memorable lyrics and music.

punk rock—A loud and fast style of music generally thought to be rebellious in nature.

record producer—A person who oversees and often directs the recording of a musical project.

royalty—A share of the profits made from a recording or other piece of work.

slam dancing—An often violent form of dancing where dancers push and shove other dancers, generally while listening to music. Also known as moshing.

stage diving—The act of getting on stage while a band is playing and jumping off, hoping to be caught by the crowd.

Further Reading

Azerrad, Michael. *Come As You Are: The Story of Nirvana*. New York: Main Street Books, Doubleday, 1993.

Berkenstadt, Jim, and Charles Cross. *Nevermind: Nirvana*. New York: Schirmer Books, 1998.

Bingham, Jane. *Heroin*. Chicago: Heinemann Library, 2006.

Borzillo, Carrie. *Nirvana: The Day-By-Day Eyewitness Chronicle*. New York: Thunder's Mouth Press, 2000.

Brite, Poppy Z. *Courtney Love*. New York: Simon & Schuster, 1997.

Cobain, Kurt. *Journals*. New York: Riverhead Books, 2002.

Crisafulli, Chuck. *Teen Spirit: The Stories Behind Every Nirvana Song*. New York: Thunder's Mouth Press, 2003.

Cross, Charles. *Heavier Than Heaven: A Biography of Kurt Cobain*. New York: Hyperion, 2001.

Halperin, Ian, and Max Wallace. *Who Killed Kurt Cobain? The Mysterious Death of an Icon*. Secaucus, N.J.: Birch Lane Press, 1998.

Martin, Michael. *Kurt Cobain*. Mankato, Minn.: Capstone Press, 2005.

Wallerstein, Claire. *Teen Suicide*. Chicago: Heinemann Library, 2003.

Internet Addresses

The Internet Nirvana Fan Club
<http://www.nirvanaclub.com/index.php?sc=2?>

Kurt Cobain Memorial Committee
<http://www.kurtcobainmemorial.org>

Nirvana Live Guide
<http://www.nirvanaguide.com>

Tom Grant's Kurt Cobain Murder Investigation
<http://www.cobaincase.com>

Selected Discography of Kurt Cobain

Albums

Bleach (Sub Pop, 1989)
Nevermind (DGC, 1991)
Incesticide (DGC, 1992)
In Utero (DGC, 1993)
MTV Unplugged In New York (DGC, 1994)
From The Muddy Banks Of The Wishkah (DGC, 1996)
Nirvana (DGC, 2002)
With The Lights Out box set, 3 CDs, 1 DVD (DGC, 2004)
Sliver: The Best of the Box (DGC, 2005)

Singles

"Love Buzz"/"Big Cheese" (Sub Pop, 1988)
"Blew"/"Love Buzz"/"Been a Son"/"Stain" (Tupelo, 1989)
"Sliver"/"Dive" (Sub Pop, 1990)
"Molly's Lips," split single with "Candy" by Fluid (Sub Pop, 1991)
"Here She Comes Now," split single with Melvins' "Venus in Furs" (Communion, 1991)
"Smells Like Teen Spirit" with "Even in His Youth" and "Aneurysm" (DGC, 1991)
"Come As You Are" with "School" (live) and "Drain You" (live) (DGC, 1992)
"Lithium" with "Been a Son" (live), "D-7" and

"Curmudgeon" (DGC, 1992)

"In Bloom" with "Polly" (live) and "Sliver" (live) (Geffen, 1992, UK only)

"In Bloom" with "Sliver" (live) (Geffen, 1992)

"Oh, the Guilt," split single with "Puss" by Jesus Lizard (Touch and Go, 1993)

"Heart-Shaped Box"/"Marigold" (written and sung by Dave Grohl) (Geffen, 1993, UK release)

"All Apologies"/"Rape Me" (Geffen, 1993, UK release)

"About a Girl"/"Something in the Way" (Geffen, 1994)

Songs on compilations

"Spank Thru," *Sub Pop 200* (Sup Pop, 1988)

"Mexican Seafood," *Teriyaki Asthma* (C/Z, 1989)

"Do You Love Me?," *Hard to Believe Kiss tribute album* (C/Z, 1990)

"Here She Comes Now," *Heaven and Hell Vol.* (Communion, 1991)

"Beeswax," *Kill Rock Stars* (Kill Rock Stars, 1991)

"Dive," *The Grunge Years* (Sub Pop, 1991)

"Return of the Rat," *Eight Songs for Greg Sage and the Wipers* (Tim Kerr Records, 1992)

"I Hate Myself and Want to Die," *The Beavis and Butt-head Experience* (Geffen, 1993)

"Sappy," *No Alternative*, hidden track (Arista, 1993)

"Pay to Play," *DGC Rarities Vol. 1* (DGC, 1994)

"Radio Friendly Unit Shifter," *Home Alive: The Art of Self Defense* (Epic, 1996)

"Rape Me" *Saturday Night Live: The Musical Performances, Vol. 2* (Dreamworks, 1999)

Index